HOW TO
ASTRO-ANALYSE
YOURSELF AND OTHERS

Provides a complete home study course in applied astrology.

HOW TO ASTRO-ANALYSE YOURSELF AND OTHERS

by

M. E. Coleman, B.A., LL.B.

Illustrated by Ellena Clews

THE AQUARIAN PRESS
Wellingborough, Northamptonshire

First published February 1985
Second Impression November 1985

British Library Cataloguing in Publication Data

Coleman, Mary Elen
   How to astro-analyse yourself and others.
   1. Astrology and psychology
   2. Personality
   I. Title
   133.5   BF1729.P8

ISBN 0-85030-400-8

*The Aquarian Press is part of the
Thorsons Publishing Group*

Printed in Great Britain by
Richard Clay (The Chaucer Press) Ltd.,
Bungay, Suffolk

CONTENTS

INTRODUCTION

WHAT THIS BOOK CAN DO FOR YOU

Let's start with a few straight questions: Do you really want to understand yourself and those you care about better? To discover why you do the things you do? To plan your life instead of just letting it all happen? To learn just what makes people fall in and out of love? To use your individual talents and minimize your failings? In short, do you want to make the most of yourself and your relationships?

This book will show you how to find workable answers to the conundrums of life, love and sex—where I did: through the study of the techniques of astro-analysis, the science which blends the ancient doctrines of astrology with the most modern methods of psychological analysis. And you don't have to be a brilliant mathematician or a budding clairvoyant to learn them. The mathematics required for calculation are not difficult and in my view clairvoyance or fortune-telling have no place whatsoever in accurate astrological analysis.

Perhaps you've already tried to study various branches of astrology before and given up in despair after running across the confusing array of different techniques and chart construction methods suggested by various textbook authors? No worries on that point with this book! Difficulties only arise if your initial instruction is not sufficiently straightforward, thorough and explicit. And here you'll find all you need to know set out in easy-to-follow, step-by-step stages.

Perhaps you've always wanted to learn astrology but been

bothered about the calculations involved? No problem there either! This book offers simple birth computation forms which are virtually mistake-proof. And to the best of my knowledge it is the very first astro-analysis textbook written by a university-qualified Australian psychologist.

What's more, you are already half-way to success when you begin to read these pages because you have revealed that you have the most important requirement for success—the genuine desire to learn what human personality is all about. Psychologically speaking, this attitude is termed motivation and strong motivation is the driving force behind every human achievement, great or small, epoch-making or everyday.

Of course, there'll be moments when your determination will flag, when you won't want to be bothered. Stay with your learning programme. Gradually, during the coming weeks as you master the techniques of astro-analysis, you'll discover a new more confident 'you' emerging. And the path to a happier, more satisfying future opening out before you.

The following chapters will teach you how to calculate, erect and interpret any horoscope chart quickly, precisely and accurately, thus revealing the answers to the riddles of your own personality and the personalities of your family, friends and associates. But some students want more personal tuition than most books can supply, which is why I decided to give my readers the opportunity to check their progress through each section by means of a set of additional home study exercises. Model answers are given with each exercise. So if you go wrong, you can check at once how and why.

WHAT ASTRO-ANALYSIS IS AND ISN'T

When, as a university-qualified psychologist, I set out to research the contemporary scene many years ago, for a time I trod the solemn and notably primrose-less path of academic enquiry. Then I happened on three thought-provoking quotes—one from ancient Greek physician Hippocrates, one from American philosopher, Ralph Waldo Emerson and one from Swiss psychologist, Carl Jung.

All were giants in their own field; all maintained that the date, place and time of a man's birth were highly significant in evaluating his reactions.

Surely they didn't mean what most people think of as astrology? All that stuff about lucky days, lucky numbers, lucky colours? No, it wasn't that. I checked further and found the only aspect of astrology these men of learning and science were concerned with was its value as a method of personality analysis.

Then I was introduced through the works of American biologist Joseph Goodavage, French statistician Michel Gauquelin and American psychologists Stephen Arroyo and Noel Tyl to a new approach which combined the ancient rules of astrological analysis with modern methods of personality evaluation and which is now being used extensively overseas. Their results amazed me. I followed up the technique, compiled basic traits for the twelve birth sign cycles, checked generation characteristics, examined associated behaviour patterns and tried it out. It worked. Within reasonable limits, I found I could anticipate reactions, and decide in advance when opposition was necessary and would get results, or when discretion was clearly better. Better still, results of astroanalytical evaluation proved as consistent and often more revealing than conventional methods of personality testing.

Indeed when I first began research into astrological techniques I realized that standard forms of personality testing were frequently disappointing and unreliable. Often because test candidates tried to anticipate the 'right' answers and gave these instead of the true ones. The motive was not deliberate deception—just that natural human desire to show the self in the most attractive light. On the other hand, the more horoscope analyses I did—the greater became my convictions that a meticulously calculated horoscope, interpreted by a properly trained analyst, *cannot* give incorrect answers.

The professional technique set out in this book is a very far cry from 'pop' astrology and does not concern itself with newspaper column type trivia—such as 'Good day to take a lottery ticket' or 'Have a party tonight'. Instead the in-depth personality portrait the chart builds up is complete, amazingly detailed and always frank. The future trends of the life pattern it indicates are equally accurate—provided you are not expecting the 'You'll meet a tall, dark stranger on 5 June' routine. That type of thing is pure fortune-telling. Astrological charting of future years is pure scientific deduction, calculated mathematically from the movements of the planets.

Remember too, from the psychological standpoint, it has been demonstrated for more than 100 years that early home environment, parental attitudes and heredity develop or distort inborn traits. Each chart will show where and how.

From the astrological standpoint, it has been demonstrated for more than 3,000 years that while the natal sun—which is what you use when you call yourself an Aries, for example—is the largest fragment in the jigsaw of human personality, its effects can be greatly modified by those of the moon, the eight planets, and the Ascendant.

This last-named (which cannot be mathematically calculated unless the actual birthtime is known or determined by a complex method called 'rectification') holds the initial answer to the oft-repeated complaint 'I've got two Leo friends and they're as different as chalk and cheese,' as you'll see later in this book. They aren't, of course! An analysis of the said two friends will invariably show they share a very large number of similar traits. The factors which make them *appear* dissimilar are a different Ascendant and other planetary positions, since these influences affect physical appearance and the overall expression of each personality.

From all this, you can see that any modern astrological analysis technique (when applied by qualified practitioners) in no way relies on clairvoyance, the supernatural, magical formulae or fortune-telling tricks. It is a plain, no-nonsense system of scientific deduction. Certainly, its methods can within clearly prescribed limits predict the future trends of a life, because as Einstein once said: 'I do what my nature drives me to do.' That applies to all of us.

Thus if you understand anyone's true nature, you will be better able to forecast how he or she will react to future events. Granted, any serious faith in astrology requires the acceptance of its ancient and basic tenets: firstly, that man is part of the infinite cosmos, and, secondly, that the positions and movements of the celestial bodies influence his life on this earth. But that is the end of the 'faith' bit. Accept that and the rest is pure factual analysis.

In Chapter 1, we'll examine in depth the behavioural responses of the twelve signs of the zodiac. Do not skip this data, even if you think you know the meanings of the signs by heart! The signs themselves represent the rock on which the vast and ancient edifice of astrological doctrine has been built. Do not skim specific sign data because you assume you have no Aries in your chart, for example. *Every one of the signs will manifest as an energy somewhere in every individual's chart.*

It might be dominant—say, four planets in Aries. It might be slight—say, the cusp of an empty fifth house. But it is always present. That is why the visual symbol and especial influence of all twelve must be thoroughly understood at the outset of your studies in astrology. Each one is a signpost directing you along the road which leads to both accuracy and success in chart interpretation.

1.

HOW TO START
YOUR ASTRO-ANALYSIS

UNDERSTANDING THE SIGNS OF THE ZODIAC

Study carefully the twelve birthdate cycles of the year and their meanings set out hereafter. These were first recorded thousands of years before the birth of Christ by ancient mystics who assigned to each cycle a specific symbol in both hieroglyphic and graphic form. The graphics are, of course, the familiar zodiacal figures such as the Lion and the Crab. You might be surprised to know that none of these figures was chosen at random or as a bit of whimsy. Each was and is intended to give an instant, composite mental picture of the personality type to which it applies, plus the key to understanding that personality. The shorthand symbol of the sign, also set out hereafter, is known as the *glyph*—as in hiero*glyphic*.

Incidentally, you'll note—if you're a regular reader of astrology—that individuals born during a specific birthdate cycle are often described as a 'Leo' or a 'Cancer', as the case may be. These terms (and the other ten) are the Latin-derived names for the zodiacal figures which have been handed down to us from Classical times.

For the purposes of astro-analysis, I have used, where possible, the English names to focus attention on the zodiacal figure itself and to ensure you evoke the correct mental picture of it. In cases of people born on the borderline (termed the *cusp*) of two signs, they will exhibit some traits of each sign. If the birth occurred within a day either way of this cusp, you have to consider the combined influence of both signs.

You may also have noted that the date cycles sometimes appear to cover slightly different periods when published in popular magazines or newspapers. This is caused by the fact that the sun moves slightly from year to year over the cusp, and popular astrology writers usually take an average.

The only way to be certain to which sign a cusp-born individual belongs, is to check in the planetary tables (called the ephemeris) for the specific date and year involved.

Having studied the twelve signs and their meanings, next, try to visualize as clearly as you can an image of, say a Lion and then a Crab. Think of what these two creatures suggest to you. Very different behaviour, very different ways of living? That's why it is most important that you familiarize yourself with the twelve symbols and remember to visualize the relevant one whenever you're working on an analysis. After all, to go back to our example, you'd never expect a Crab to act like a Lion, would you? Thus, it follows that you'll never make the mistake of expecting a Lion personality type to react like a Crab personality type.

You'll find detailed descriptions of the visualization and typical behavioural responses of the twelve signs in the next few pages. However, before you go on to learn each one, remember that each sign is also divided into three sub-groups or classifications, which are outlined below.

THE CLASSIFICATIONS

The polarities (also known as positivity/negativity)

(a) *Positive:* All air and all fire signs, i.e., Gemini, Libra, Aquarius; Aries, Leo, Sagittarius. Positive signs promote self-expression, extroversion, and assertion of individual will and needs.

(b) *Negative:* All earth and all water signs, i.e., Taurus, Virgo, Capricorn; Cancer, Scorpio, Pisces. Negative signs promote receptivity, introversion, and repression of individual will and needs.

The qualities (also known as the quadruplicities)

(a) *Cardinal:* Aries, Cancer, Libra and Capricorn. Cardinal signs manifest as an outgoing, active, thrusting drive, rather like the flight of a spear. Hold this *spear-like* image firmly in your mind when you think of cardinal signs and you'll understand how each one demonstrates, in its individual way, a forceful, enterprising approach. Wherever you find cardinal signs in a chart is precisely where the self strives to express most assertively. A predominance of cardinal signs in any chart implies an individual with a strong, instinctive sense of goals and objectives. Or to put it in a nutshell, cardinals know where they're going!

(b) *Fixed:* Taurus, Leo, Scorpio and Aquarius. Fixed signs manifest as a steadfast, immovable, stubborn stance, rather like a massive rock, embedded in soil. Hold this *rock-like* image firmly in your mind when you think of fixed signs and you'll understand how each one demonstrates, in its individual way, an unbending, immovable approach. Wherever you find fixed signs in a chart is precisely where the self will refuse to be budged from its standpoint. A predominance of fixed signs in any chart implies an individual with gut confidence and faith in his/her own convictions—even in the face of contrary evidence. Or to put it in a nutshell, fixeds dig their heels in!

(c) *Mutable:* Gemini, Virgo, Sagittarius and Pisces. Mutable signs manifest as a restless, changeable, adaptable bent, rather like bamboos bending before a wind. Hold this *bamboo-like* image firmly in your mind when you think of mutable signs and you'll understand how each one demonstrates, in its individual way, a flexible, amenable approach. Wherever you find mutable signs in a chart is precisely where the self will give way and see the other side of the question. A predominance of mutable signs in any chart implies an individual who will roll with punches, flow with the tide. Or to put it in a nutshell, mutables change their hats to suit the scene!

Always remember that the above qualities of cardinality, fixity or mutability express in accordance with the sign of the zodiac to which they apply. (See following section.) As you'll soon observe, Aries, Cancer, Libra and Capricorn are all cardinal signs and thus all exhibit a powerful ego thrust, but aim it in different directions. For example, the sometimes glaring egocentricity of Aries is so obvious, no one can mistake it. Yet the subtle, undeviating power drive of Capricorn can turn others into stepping-stones before they realize it.

The elements (also known as the triplicities)

(a) *Fire:* Aries, Leo, Sagittarius. Fire signs exhibit an instinctive reaction to stimuli that is fast, impulsive and vigorous—in fact, fiery. Fire is a hot, volatile element, hence full of enthusiasm, quick-on-the-draw, vital and warming. Fire rushes up with a roar—like an igniting flame—but often burns out just as swiftly. Fire appears exciting but it can scorch and consume all around it.

(b) *Air:* Gemini, Libra, Aquarius. Air signs exhibit an instinctive reaction to stimuli, that is light, intellectualized and detached—an 'airy' response. Air is a cool, blowing element, hence flying high, seeing all things through the bright lens of the intellect. Air loves words, concepts, ideas but is uncomfortable in the world of feeling and emotion. Air appears stimulating but—like a whirlwind—it can blow all before it away.

(c) *Earth:* Taurus, Virgo, Capricorn. Earth signs exhibit an instinctively 'earthy' reaction to stimuli: prudent, cautious and realistic. Earth is a hard, solid element, hence steadfast, dependable, calm and supportive. Earth is as real as the ground under foot, but is often just as flat and unyielding. Earth loves working, making and doing things but dislikes the spontaneous, the unexpected. Earth appears strong, but it can cave in under pressure.

(d) *Water:* Cancer, Scorpio, Pisces. Water signs exhibit an instinctive reaction to stimuli that is deep, emotional and reflective—watery. Water is a deep, wet element, hence full of undercurrents, moody, flowing and responsive. Water cools and refreshes but often overwhelms with the tides of emotion. Water appears understanding but it can—like a whirlpool—drown all else in its depths.

You'll appreciate the effect of the elemental patterns in personality if you always visualize each element as you consider it, because astrology is fundamentally a language of symbols.

Think of each element as it *is* in nature. Then you'll grasp instantly why each symbolizes something different:

Fire	Passions
Air	Intellect
Earth	Senses
Water	Emotions

THE TWELVE BASIC HUMAN PERSONALITIES

Quick-reference data

1. Aries—Ram
2. Taurus—Bull
3. Gemini—Twins
4. Cancer—Crab
5. Leo—Lion
6. Virgo—Virgin
7. Libra—Scales
8. Scorpio—Scorpion
9. Sagittarius—Centaur
10. Capricorn—Goat
11. Aquarius—Water-Bearer
12. Pisces—Fish

ARIES . . . Sign of the Ram

Winning is the name of every game for typical Ram personalities. Their energy is legendary. Competition is the breath of life and 'me, myself and I' are the most important pronouns in the Chief Sheep vocabulary.

1. Aries: The Ram ♈

21 March-20 April. Planetary ruler: Mars. Behavioural key phrases: 'I am'. Classification: Cardinal—Fire—Positive.

Visualization

Male sheep, medium-sized animal, designed by Nature to lead the flock, to fight off anyone who might endanger it, usurp his leadership or threaten any ewe or lamb in his charge.

Their life-style

Ram personalities live in a constant state of paradox. They're rash but conventional. Remember, despite those dangerous-looking horns, they are still sheep.

They're idealistic but hard-headed. They'll thunder off anywhere in pursuit of a dream as long as someone bigger than them hasn't locked the paddock gate.

They'll lead you to believe they're the eighth wonder of the world but deep in their psyches doubt every word they tell you.

Their angle

Abrupt in manner, arrogant in conduct, shatteringly frank in speech, they charge their way through their day and don't even notice if they trample down a daisy or two in transit.

Their problems

The only thing which really throws them is inner conflict, those times when the self-doubt that's always there beneath the braggadocio rears its ugly head. Then they become nervous, timid, halting—just another sheep.

Their attitude

Typical Ram personalities have minds that go with their passion for rushing in where angels fear to tread. With them, daredevil courage, split-second decisions, bright ideas and competition are the breath of life.

Individual expertise, speed and 'putting the personality over positively' are the Ram's answer to everybody's problems. Solid teamwork or plodding through statistics is strictly for also-rans. Action is the Ram's motivating force.

Never try to play the 'heavy' with Ram personalities. They can't bear taking orders, uncommunicative friends, or layabouts.

Their symbol
The curly-horned, charging *leader of the flock*.

TAURUS . . . Sign of the Bull

Committed sensualists of beautiful simplicity, typical Bull personalities put first things first . . . i.e., the acquisition of a comfortable domain in which to stroll while smelling the flowers and/or rolling in the clover.

2. Taurus: The Bull ♉

21 April-21 May. Planetary ruler: Venus: Behavioural key phrase: 'I have'. Classification: Fixed—Earth—Negative.

Visualization
Male bovine, large animal of ruminant habits, domesticated since prehistoric times, designed by Nature to guide small personal harem of cows (plus calves) over long distances in search of suitable

fodder, pausing only to gore to death anything at all that impedes their peaceful progress.

Their life-style

Bull personalities are committed sensualists of beautiful simplicity. All they ask is a satisfying partner for the regular rolls in the clover, a comfortable domain in which to stroll and smell the flowers, and a regular supply of good, plain food. Granted these home-spun pleasures, they'll go quietly with never so much as a snort—let alone a bellow. But cross them, coerce them or try to fence them in and you'll wonder what started the earthquake.

Their angle

No one could describe them as selfish but they can be very stubborn and detest being contradicted. (Pig-headedness has nothing on bull-headedness on such occasions!) Slightly ponderous in manner, persistent in conduct, slow of speech, they work each patch of pasture over with tranquil application and can always be relied upon to find the family herd an oasis in the driest desert.

Their problems

In fact, the only cloud on their personality horizon is their dormant but nonetheless real capacity for sudden blind rage. (Remember the old saying about the bull in a china shop?) Then they become violent, destructive, terrible—satisfied with nothing less than total demolition.

Their attitude

Typical Bull personalities have minds that go with the calm, comfortable, simple life in which there is always time to pause and watch the grass grow. Speed is an anathema, flustering them to the point where they truly charge around in circles. Thoroughness is their pride and joy.

Not that they're dullards or slowcoaches. They'll work on solid, worthwhile, durable projects with a tenacity of purpose that has to be seen to be believed. Slapdash efforts produce a snort of disapproval. *Construction* is the Bull's motivating force.

Never try to push or hustle Bull personalities. They can't bear ugly surroundings, fair-weather friends or pushy, restless people.

Their symbol
The long-horned, stalwart *protector of the herd*.

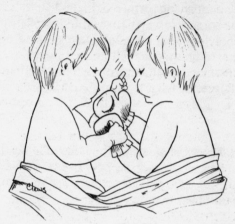

GEMINI . . . Sign of the Twins

Inevitably adding up to double trouble for single-minded souls, typical Twins personalities, whatever their chronological age, never lose their air of youthful curiosity about what makes the world and everything in it tick.

3. Gemini: The Twins ♊

22 May—21 June. Planetary ruler: Mercury. Behavioural key phrase: 'I think'. Classification: Mutable—Air—Positive.

Visualization
Male twins, half god, half mortal, identical in appearance, opposite in temperament—but that's not all. The zodiac's particular pair are a very special breed of twins, the progeny of none other than Greek god Zeus and Spartan queen Leda (who is also famed as the mother of Helen of Troy). Zeus is variously renowned for his prowess at thunderbolt throwing, meting out instant justice and

fading into the mountain greenery with anything nubile.

Their life-style

Twin personalities live by the theory that two heads are better than one. They've got to! Because they actually do *have* twin personalities, both as different as chalk and cheese. Indeed, this duality (with the inevitable changeability it creates) is such an integral part of them that they automatically add up to double trouble for any ordinary person trying to understand them. As a result, even their nearest and dearest find phrases like 'two-faced' and 'two-timing' tend to leap to the lips sometimes. But that's not strictly fair. They don't deliberately set out to bamboozle.

Their angle

Quick with their wits, alert, sympathetic and affable, they can talk their way out of a whole row of paper bags and—whatever their chronological age—never ever lose their air of youthful let's-have-a-party type enthusiasm.

Their problems

As long as the sun's shining and gay, gregarious Twin Number One's in charge—they're everybody's friend. But let the storm clouds gather and the first flash of lightning will often reveal the self-centred, chilly, disgruntled profile of Twin Number Two.

Their attitude

Typical Twin personalities have minds that fit their insatiable urge for new places, people and ideas. Mentally and physically restless, pulled this way and that by the conflicting stimuli of their twin minds, they are facile and ambidextrous.

Short-term learning appeals. Long-term study appalls. This attitude is their Achilles heel. They skim over the surface of life, winning their way with their quick, double-edged wits, chatting glibly and gaily, appearing and disappearing on the scene with the ease of a Cheshire cat! *Versatility* is the Twin's motivating force.

They can't bear hung-up characters, slow minds or dreamy, illogical reasoning. Never try to clip the intellectual wings of Twin personalities.

Their symbol
The dual-bodied, dual-minded *heavenly twins*.

CANCER . . . Sign of the Crab

Home-bodies and parents *par excellence*, typical Crab personalities like nothing better than to submerge in a cavern of mutual devotion with their nearest and dearest while the workaday world makes its waves overhead.

4. Cancer: The Crab ♋
22 June—23 July. Planetary ruler: Moon. Behavioural key phrase: 'I feel'. Classification: Cardinal—Water—Negative.

Visualization
Ten-legged crustacean, small creature of aquatic habits found mainly in tidal pools, rock crevices and along sea shores. Instantly identifiable by heavily armoured shell, encasing vital organs and all fleshy parts. Designed by Nature to lead a solitary life, eating and defending itself by use of two giant, anterior nipper-like claws. When threatened or provoked takes one of two possible courses of action—either clamps adversary in claws and hangs on grimly or scrambles for cover by using its ten legs in quick, darting, sideways movements.

Their life-style

Crab personalities live in a swirling sea of emotions, which sweep them along—ebbing and flowing, rising and falling like the tides of the ocean. But until you *really* know them, you'd never suspect it! For day in, day out, silent and alone in their glossy, well-accoutred shell, apparently impervious to the storms and cross-currents raging around them, they go about their daily business with quiet tenacity. Not for them the swashbuckling swagger, or the do-or-die, hell-or-glory dash. They rarely make a direct approach to anyone or anything. Instead they pause, calculate the odds and come at their goal sideways, usually from an angle you wouldn't imagine existed.

Their angle

Slightly gruff in manner, immediately sensitive to atmosphere, careful of speech, they pick their way over the rocks of life with judicious caution. Always prudent, sometimes ruthless but never reckless, they have a strong sense of duty and whether employer or employee they give and expect a good day's work for a good day's pay.

Their problem

The only thing that stops them in their tracks and sends them darting for cover is an unexpected encounter with a stranger whose perspicacity is sharp enough to spot the chink in all that well-shone armour. Then their response is a very crabby curtness.

Their attitude

Typical Crab personalities have minds which operate through a tough, undentable surface, concealing exceptional softness of heart. They can immerse themselves absolutely in work or play with unwavering determination. Yet because of a deep need for acceptance and recognition (and despite innate shyness) they never become backroom types. Limelight lures them like a far-off beacon: tenacity of purpose assures its attainment, provided not too much muscle is called for. *Tenacity* is the Crab's motivating force.

They can't bear inquisitive strangers, capricious minds or

untrustworthy people. Never neglect or rebuff Crab personalities.

Their symbol
The hard-shelled, giant-nippered *Ocean Crab*.

LEO . . . Sign of the Lion

Possessed of an unwavering faith in the Divine Right of Kings . . . as long as they're King and they're right . . . typical Lion personalities consider themselves Lords of the Concrete Jungle, as well as the palm-fringed variety.

5. Leo: The Lion ♌

24 July-23 August. Planetary ruler: Sun. Behavioural key phrase: 'I will'. Classification: Fixed—Fire—Positive.

Visualization

Male feline, large carnivore of dignified appearance and lazy disposition, generally known as the 'King of the Beasts'. Associated with royal households and regarded as a royal animal from the beginning of recorded history. Designed by Nature to direct small retinue of subordinate lionesses, plus adolescent and infant cubs on daily stalking sorties. Protocol is strict and requires lionesses to pursue, catch, kill and deposit meal (untasted) at their sovereign master's feet. He does not exert himself except to yawn, dine, roar, reproduce the royal line or despatch potential threats to the throne.

Their life-style

Lion personalities are benevolent despots of magnificent proportions—often in every sense of the phrase.

They have an unwavering faith in: the divine right of kings (as long as they're King or Queen and they're right); inequality of the classes (why be a monarch and do your own work?); the value of pomp and circumstance (provided they're the circumstance the pomp is all about).

Their angle

Lordly in manner, commanding in conduct, slightly patronizing in speech and heavy-handed with both brickbats and bouquets, they make their royal progress through their special corner of the asphalt jungle daily, graciously accepting cheers and accolades, blissfully unaware of the corns they amble over.

Their problems

Indeed, it is this supreme faith in their own superiority and strength which is their greatest weakness. Inevitably it leaves them open to persuasion by flattery and can make them behave pompously and snobbishly, which in turn leads to wrong decisions and foolish posturing. It is at times like these that they realize just *how* uneasy lies the head that wears the crown!

Their attitude

Typical Lion personalities have minds which go with their high, wide and handsome life-style. Physically, too, there is often something of the big cat about them—tawny colouring, a broad-shouldered, slim-hipped body or an unhurried 'padding' walk.

They are never mean-spirited or petty, often generous to the point of lunatic extravagance, given to moments of most endearing clowning. Lion personalities love to be loved and often are—for those reasons.

Sovereignty is the Lion's motivating force.

They can't bear inhibited characters, being dictated to or 'loner' type amusements. Never try to play 'Top Cat' with Lion personalities.

Their symbol
The dignified, regal *king of the jungle*.

VIRGO . . . Sign of the Virgin

Cool-hearted, clear-minded and disconcertingly diligent, typical Virgin personalities really would rather work than play. They are always thinking about the next task, working at it or sleeping to gather up enough energy to get on with it.

6. Virgo: The Virgin ♍

24 August-23 September. Planetary ruler: Mercury. Behavioural key phrase: 'I analyse'. Classification: Mutable—Earth—Negative.

Visualization

Before you start, understand that this is the only date cycle of the entire twelve represented by a female symbol—but don't let that fool you into thinking it means that the men born during this period are effeminate or the women soft. In antiquity, when the symbol was chosen, the young virgin epitomized purity of mind, perfection of body and self-sacrifice—often of a gruesomely literal nature.

The zodiac's particular virgin is depicted as a goddess-like, golden-haired maiden, garbed in flowing robes of classical white, bearing in one hand the wheatsheaf of fertility to indicate the close kinship to the ancient deities of earth and harvest, together with the eternal promise that those who labour faithfully shall reap their rightful rewards.

Their life-style

Virgin personalities are permanently suspended—like Mohammed's coffin—betwixt earth and heaven. They're purists *par excellence*, but far below those lofty windswept peaks which their souls inhabit stand feet of clay, each with an Achilles heel. They're an all-the-way, mind-over-matter type, but whereas the mind is cool as a crystal pool, the matter is solid earth.

Their angle

Basically loners, they usually look for occupations where they have only to rely on their own impeccable judgement. Professions like law, medicine and journalism thus appeal. Here, too, their naturally deferential approach to the 'powers that be' helps.

Slightly reserved in manner, down-to-earth in conduct, quick but sparing of speech, they offer up all they've got—their formidable talents, their great industry, their keen intellect—upon the twin altars of Wisdom and Truth and so rarely fail in any of their multifarious endeavours. (Heaven *does* protect the working girl or boy!)

Their problems
Sadly, the absolute dedication and discrimination of Virgin personalities don't exactly encourage close friendships or warm communication. They'll calmly think their way (and yours) out of most kinds of trouble but they're anything but a barrel of laughs.

Their attitude
Typical Virgin personalities have minds that fit their neat, trim and immaculate appearance. Cool-hearted, clear-minded and incredibly diligent, they methodically pursue chosen objectives with quiet dedication.

Their recreations are invariably some other form of work. Most are born scholars because productive learning exercises a lifelong attraction.

Discrimination is the Virgin's motivating force. They can't bear airy-fairy characters, pretentious behaviour or pomposity.

Never push Virgin personalities into accepting second-best efforts or second-best relationships.

Their symbol
The white-robed, golden-haired *perfect maiden*.

7. Libra: The Scales ♎

24 September-23 October. Planetary ruler: Venus. Behavioural key phrase: 'I balance'. Classification: Cardinal—Air—Positive.

Visualization
Pair of golden scales, expertly assembled according to the specifications of classical design, comprising two identical weighing pans, suspended from central beam by slender rods and perpetually poised in the position of absolute equality. Movement is restricted to simple up or down motion. Most significant of all is the fact that this date cycle is the only one of the twelve represented by an inanimate machine instead of by a living creature.

LIBRA . . . Sign of the Scales

Ever ready to act the part of 'Dove of Peace' in love or war, typical Scales personalities are natural diplomats who weigh up the pros and cons with consummate skill and balance their way out of the blood-thirstiest battles.

Their life-style
Scales personalities function with the perfect predictability of a beautiful but unsophisticated mechanical device. The same mechanistic attitude, with its concomitant dislike of change and its need for someone else to get the ideas and press the starter buttons, nevertheless keeps them running very smoothly as long as nothing untoward happens and no one throws a spanner into the works.

Their angle
It also goes without saying that Scales personalities have a natural affinity with the philosophies and pressures against individualism of the Space Age, and often an eerily intuitive understanding of machines.

Agreeable in manner, tactful in conduct, never vehemently partisan in speech, they genuinely strive to balance the scales of life and smooth the onrush of a calm, comfortable, civilized world.

Their problems
The only defect in their infinite and invaluable capacity for sifting, weighing and stabilizing is their tendency to vacillate and the intrinsic superficiality of their judgements and attachments. Because they see but rarely feel, they are not 'equipped' to understand that human responses are frequently inharmonious, often unbalanced with pride or passion, and cannot ever be stacked up tidily on either side of the golden scales.

Their attitude
Typical Scales personalities have minds that work like a perfectly tuned machine plus an elegant, well-kept but unobtrusive appearance. Their predilection for calm assessment attracts them to civilized occupations.

Harmony is the Scales motivating force.

They can't bear discourteous people, freakish attitudes or 'going-it-alone'.

Never be inconsistent or unjust with Scales personalities.

Their symbol
The gleaming, ever-balancing *set of golden scales*.

8. Scorpio: The Scorpion ♏
24 October-22 November. Planetary ruler: Pluto. Behavioural key phrase: 'I desire'. Classification: Fixed—Water—Negative.

Visualization
Eight-legged, nocturnal arachnid; large, shiny insect, designed by Nature to lead solitary life hunting by night and resting during day under stones or in deep burrows; characterized by long, segmented tail which terminates in the distinctive and sinister venom-bearing hook. This lethal extremity is habitually carried arched upwards over the back to display it at its most intimidating—thus challenging friend and foe alike.

SCORPIO . . . Sign of the Scorpion

Out of sight is out of mind is a rule typical Scorpion personalities live by. They'll conceal both their intentions and themselves under anything handy—watching and waiting till the moment comes to leap out and strike.

Their life-style
Scorpion personalities are penultimate extremists who live on the ever-crumbling edges of a precipice. They are always their own men or women, the author of a brilliant destiny or the tragic, yet sinister, self-executioner, dying in pursuit of the impossible dream. Born to be misunderstood, loved or hated but never ignored, they act with a ruthless intensity which rarely counts the cost to themselves or to others. With them there are no half measures, no compromises and no loose ends. It's all or nothing at all—from here to eternity.

Their angle
Predictably, because of their deep and secret minds, Scorpion personalities work in mysterious ways their wonders to perform. Predictably, too, this mind predisposes them towards the occult, to reliance on hunches and intuitive flashes and often to the

investigation of strange and off-beat religious experiences. Inscrutable in manner, bold in conduct, curt in speech, they perpetually pit themselves against irresistible forces and immovable objects armed with nothing but the lash of their will and the sting of their words.

Their problems
The only defect in their powerful and compelling personality is their refusal to trust any leadership but their own and their desire to revenge themselves on those who wrong or oppose them. Because they think and feel with equal intensity, they are loyal friends and are blood-curdling enemies. Belitted or betrayed, they will not hesitate to create a cataclysm so final it will destroy their whole world *and* themselves.

Their attitude
Typical Scorpion personalities have minds and bodies that go with their indomitable wills. Usually highly intelligent, they apply themselves with silent determination to the achievement of their private dreams and never leave a stone unturned in pursuit of the goal. The rougher the competition, the more they thrive. For the Scorpion, winning is the name of every game. *Victory* is the Scorpion's motivating force.

They can't bear professional sweeties, two-timers or stuffy, formal parties.

Never deliberately deceive Scorpion personalities or make them promises you can't keep.

Their symbol
The silent, solitary *sting-tailed Scorpion*.

SAGITTARIUS . . . Sign of the Centaur

Avowed enthusiasts for all kinds of athletic action, typical Centaur personalities dash through life at a thundering gallop. Never hesitant when it comes to taking a sporting chance, the race is always for the excitement—not the gold cups.

9. Sagittarius: The Centaur ♐

23 November-22 December. Planetary ruler: Jupiter. Behavioural key phrase: 'I see'. Classification: Mutable—Fire—Positive.

Visualization

Male hybrid, half man, half horse, member of a fabled race of huge, magnificently proportioned but savage creatures, famed for their skill in snatching nubile maidens while thundering across the countryside at full gallop. The zodiac's particular centaur always appears as a handsome, bearded and muscular man, human to the waist only, while the rest of his body is that of a great, shaggy-haired stallion. His fingers constantly aim a drawn bow and arrow at the highest heaven.

Their life-style

Centaur personalities are creatures divided against themselves—in both the literal and metaphorical senses of the term. Their instincts are crude, easily satisfied and unbridled. (They emanate from the horse half!) Their thoughts are noble, high-minded and pure. (They emanate from the human half!) Their actions can be dictated by either half or by both halves together. (This can be clumsy at best, mind-boggling at worst!)

Their angle

Predictably, because of their high, wide and handsome attitude, Centaur personalities can often be classed as the world's best brick-droppers. Tact, delicacy or anything more than the most superficial awareness of other people's touchy spots are beyond them. Open in manner, confident in conduct, jovial in speech, they are forever aiming their arrows at the farthest star and crashing off in its wake with nothing more than their unerring eye for the main chance to guide them.

Their problems

The chief defect in their big, bold and breezy natures is their animal exuberance, which often leads them into empty boasting—to a tendency towards exaggerating even their molehills of achievement into mountains so as to obscure the fact that they've been overcome with boredom or spotted a new colt or filly in a farther field before they finish the job.

Their attitude

Typical Centaur personalities have minds that fit their favourite maxim: 'a healthy mind in a healthy body'. Most forms of athletic effort exert a lifelong attraction, particularly those connected with horses and dogs.

In work and play, they take wins and losses with equally exuberant good humour. Their sense of fair play is so highly developed, they will never trample on others to succeed. The race is always for the excitement—not the gold cups. *Enthusiasm* is the Centaur's motivating force.

They can't bear frosty manners, undemocratic people, or gloomy behaviour.

Never try to slap a harness on Centaur personalities.

Their symbol
The half-human, half-horse, *bow-and-arrow-bearing Centaur.*

CAPRICORN . . . Sign of the Goat

Onwards and upwards is the favourite motto of typical Goat personalities. They never cease their cautious, chasm-leaping climb till the loftiest summits—professional, social, emotional—are solid as the Rock of Ages beneath their well-shod feet.

10. Capricorn: The Goat ♑
23 December-20 January. Planetary ruler: Saturn. Behavioural key phrase: 'I use'. Classification: Cardinal—Earth—Negative.

Visualization

Male goat, small climbing cloven-hoofed quadruped, typified by hollow, back-swept horns and short, goatee-style beard. Designed by Nature to eke out nomadic existence in desolate, alpine pastures in which he and his herd survive and flourish through their capacity to make long, death-defying leaps from crag to crag.

Strongly family-minded, the older buck (better known as a billy-goat) stands guard over his grazing does and kids, ready to butt any would-be predators into the nearest chasm.

Their life-style

Goat personalities are individuals with one-track minds—but definitely not the usual kind! Their track is steep, stark and stony. It snakes around the frowning crags of their inordinate ambition and the yawning crevasses of their occasional misjudgements. It is narrow as a hairpin, lonely as the grave and the signpost always says 'The Way to the Top'. For 'Tops'—professional, social and emotional—are all Goats really care about. They must climb every Everest they encounter—or die in the attempt (which in fact, sometimes happens). Desire for prestige and the financial recognition of it, drive them like a goad so that they plod forever, grimly onward and upward.

Their angle

Unlike many of the other eleven personality types, Goat personalities like 'nothing that comes easy' and they're the last soul in the world who has to be warned that all that glitters is not gold. Austere, taciturn, routine-minded, they make their dogged (but still death-defying) leaps up the rocky road to success until the topmost summit is theirs and nothing stands between their spreading horns and heaven but the endless, unscaleable sky.

Their problems

By far the most materialistic of the twelve personality types, a provider without peer, they may sadly illustrate the old maxim: 'The higher they fly, the harder they fall'. For, even if they never so much as stumble on the dangerous ascent, they too often find too late that the Room at the Top is as insubstantial as the clouds which surround it.

Their attitude
Typical Goat personalities have minds that go with their strong, trim, wiry bodies. They're mentally and physically built for endurance, survival, agility. Learning appeals. Sports do not. Not that they're bookworms or milksops. Throughout their lives they never lose the same persevering, down-to-earth, punctilious approach to everything, including eating, drinking and exercising. The result: they rarely lose their shapes.

  Tradition is the Goat's motivating force.

  They can't bear being talked down to, or mixing with irresponsible, frivolous people.

  Never nag or needle Goat personalities.

Their symbol
The sure-footed, high-climbing *mountain Goat*.

11. Aquarius: The Water-Bearer ≈
21 January-19 February. Planetary ruler: Uranus. Behavioural key phrase: 'I know'. Classification: Fixed—Air—Positive.

Visualization
Human male, handsome, slimly built youth, balancing a huge, earthenware pitcher from which flows an endless cascade of sparkling water. But the zodiac's particular water-vendor is much more than an itinerant salesman. Having started life as a simple mortal, his good looks and indefatigable application to peddling his watery wares were soon noted from above, resulting in his being whisked up into the heavens to satisfy the thirst of the gods for all eternity. Most significant, too, is the fact that this date-cycle is the only one of the twelve represented by an ordinary human being.

AQUARIUS . . . Sign of the Water-Bearer

The absolute ultimate in free-thinking humanitarians, typical Water-Bearer personalities are born believers in the Brotherhood of Man and seekers after the proverbial pot of gold at the end of the cosmic rainbow.

Their life-style
Water-Bearer personalities are the original, all-fired idealists—the type who keep their feet in the clouds and their heads on the sunny side of the rainbow. They confidently expect all troubles (theirs and all humanity's) to melt away like lemon drops, and are positively shocked when they don't. They'd like to hold the whole world in their arms and teach it how to sing *and* to think *and* to love, but habitually forget that large sections of it need a guaranteed meal-ticket first.

Nevertheless, their daily disappointments with the hard facts of life never give them pause and they travel cheerily on, sprinkling the bright waters of their idealism on every parched patch of ignorance, intolerance or acquisitiveness they encounter.

Their angle
Altruistic, independent and spontaneous, Water-Bearer personalities are very much citizens of the world (or better still, the universe). They inexorably gravitate towards the highest planes of existence and float airily there, lost in their thoughts of brotherly love and dreaming their utopian dreams while the bus goes without them and the wheels of industry grind to a halt far away below.

Their problems
Bearing in mind all the foregoing, it hardly needs saying that many of their confederates regard them as eccentrically individualistic to the point of being unreal. And it is always only too easy for their ahead-of-their-time concepts and philosophies to lead them into preaching anarchy and spreading discontent.

Their attitude
Typical Water-Bearer personalities have bodies which go with their way-out, original, almost eccentrically individualistic minds. They usually have a graceful, lightly boned, slenderish build and a very distinctive, 'springy' way of walking. Their habitual expression is aloof, slightly superior but curiously sympathetic.

Neither organized sport nor slogging study have much appeal to Water-Bearers. They are always far too busy working out bigger, broader and better designs for living to learn what they instinctively know anyway. *Inventiveness* is the Water-Bearer's motivating force.

They can't bear stodgy dressing, meanness in money or spirit, or suffering fools gladly.

Never preach orthodoxy or conventional standards to Water-Bearer personalities.

Their symbol
The handsome, itinerant *bearer of the urn*.

PISCES . . . Sign of the Fish

Unworldly, unfathomable wanderers-in-wonderland, typical Fish personalities float gently on the tides of life, alternately swept offshore or in by the mysterious moods, hunches and intuitions which guide them through the depths.

12. Pisces: The Fish ✕
20 February-20 March. Planetary ruler: Neptune. Behavioural key phrase: 'I believe'. Classification: Mutable—Water—Negative.

Visualization
Pair of identical, deep-water fish, exotically coloured and shimmering faintly in the shadowy depths. The two are invisibly linked together but are forever swimming strongly in two diametrically opposite directions at once, one upstream, one downstream. The effect of this on their environment is plenty of churned-up water, billions of bubbles but no apparent progress either way. The effect of this on the fish themselves is a constant feeling of swimming up and down on the same spot.

Their life-style
Fish personalities are creatures of the depths, forever pulled this

way and that by the conflicting forces of their physical and spiritual selves. They think deeply on all kinds of abstruse, impractical problems, but aren't really interested in solving them. They love deeply in a gentle, poetic, unfathomable way, so that they float in and out of emotional entanglements on the tides of their easily touched feelings.

Their angle
Predictably, because of their idealism (which is more emotional than intellectual) Fish personalities are lifelong 'Love thy neighbour' and 'Do unto others as you would have them do unto you' types. Tentative in manner, hesitant in conduct and often vague in speech, they glide through their day with such a gentle swish that they never make a ripple or disturb the smallest anemone.

Their problems
The major defect in the delicate fabric of their sensitive and serene personality is its total lack of worldliness. Because they feel the need of others with such intensity, they are too easily swept away by (often misplaced) trust only to find themselves left with nothing but the black pool of their consequent self-pity.

Their attitude
Typical Fish personalities have minds superficially akin to their zodiacal cousin, Gemini. They exhibit the same duality, quick-change moods and hard-to-hold qualities, but are far less rational, far more sensitive, and far less involved with exteriors.

Idealism is the Fish's motivating force.

They can't bear squares in mind or dress, intolerance or go-getters. Never put a tight line on Fish personalities.

Their symbol
The elusive, bound-together *twin denizens of the deep*.

A note on the test exercises
You will test your progress most satisfactorily if you apply the following rules every time you complete your test exercises.

1. Prepare a simulated examination room atmosphere, i.e.: study each chapter thoroughly *before* you begin; do not refer to the course chapter or any other textbooks when doing the test; work alone and in a quiet room; and do not discuss questions with anyone else.
2. Time yourself, answering all questions at one sitting.
3. Keep your answers as concise and precise as you can.
4. Type your answers if possible: otherwise, ensure your handwriting is easily legible. Number answers on separate sheet of paper.
5. Don't be afraid to state your own views. Original thinking advances you faster than merely repeating the ideas of any textbook author.

TEST EXERCISES

1. The following twenty-four adjectives apply to *plus* or *minus* traits of each of the twelve signs of the zodiac. Select the two adjectives which, in your opinion, belong to each sign.

dignified	foolhardy
graceful	dogmatic
enthusiastic	hypersensitive
responsible	inconsistent
inventive	smothering
forceful	languid
imaginative	despotic
discriminating	vengeful
intense	fault-finding
versatile	plodding
protective	eccentric
persevering	improvident

2. The Sun sign represents the true self and thus markedly affects choice of occupation.

   Which of the following occupations do you think would appeal to which signs?

   (a) diver (b) farmer (c) actor (d) professional sportsman

(e) beautician (f) salesman (g) dressmaker (h) detective. Give your reasons why in each case.

3. What would be the outstanding traits you would expect to find in an individual whose chart showed a strong emphasis on *positive* signs? Define in your own words the astrological meaning of 'positivity' and 'negativity'.

4. State the differing types of behaviour you would expect from an individual with a majority of cardinal signs compared to an individual with a majority of mutable signs (a) in applying for a job; (b) in personal affairs.

5. The triplicities provoke reactions which reflect the qualities of each element. Which element would you expect to find stressed in charts of individuals who:
   (a) take a detached, intellectual view of life.
   (b) solve problems by dashing headlong at them.
   (c) are easily affected by atmosphere and emotional needs.
   (d) plot out and plan every step before taking it.
   Also give your reasons why in each case.

6. Imagine someone has just won a huge sum of money from the football pools. What would you expect each of the twelve basic personality types to do with the money?
   (a) Aries
   (b) Taurus
   (c) Gemini
   (d) Cancer
   (e) Leo
   (f) Virgo
   (g) Libra
   (h) Scorpio
   (i) Sagittarius
   (j) Capricorn
   (k) Aquarius
   (l) Pisces

7. What problems would you anticipate in a marriage or permanent relationship between two individuals who show in their respective charts:
   (a) a majority of planets in water? (male partner)
       a majority of planets in fire? (female partner)
   (b) a majority of planets in air? (male partner)
       a majority of planets in earth? (female partner)

8. Assume you're taking a small boy for the first day at school. How would you expect him to behave if his chart showed a strong mix of (a) positive, cardinal, air planets; (b) negative, mutable, water planets.

9. State your own Sun sign and set out which other Sun sign individuals you feel most comfortable with, then those you feel most awkward with. Explain your reasons in each case.

10. On the next four pages, you'll find a blank graph sheet for each of the twelve signs. Complete this from memory. Note the term *glyph* means the shorthand symbol of signs or planets used in chart construction. When complete and corrected, file this in your course folder for instant reference.

Sign	Symbol	Ruler	Category	Birth Cycle	Glyph
Aries					
Taurus					
Gemini					
Cancer					
Leo					
Virgo					

Sign	Symbol	Ruler	Category	Birth Cycle	Glyph
Libra					
Scorpio					
Sagittarius					
Capricorn					
Aquarius					
Pisces					

Sign	Basic Interests	Negative Traits	Positive Traits
Aries			
Taurus			
Gemini			
Cancer			
Leo			
Virgo			

Sign	Basic Interests	Negative Traits	Positive Traits	
Libra				
Scorpio				
Sagittarius				
Capricorn				
Aquarius				
Pisces				

MODEL ANSWERS

Note

The model answers given in the following pages are offered in fairly brief outline as guidance to each test participant. Your own answers do not have to be exactly the same to be marked as 'correct'. Original thinking is always rewarded, provided that your ideas show you have learned and understood the basic tenets of astrological theory.

Q1

Pluses	*Minuses*
Forceful	Foolhardy = Aries
Persevering	Plodding = Taurus
Versatile	Inconsistent = Gemini
Protective	Smothering = Cancer
Dignified	Despotic = Leo
Discriminating	Fault-finding = Virgo
Graceful	Languid = Libra
Intense	Vengeful = Scorpio
Enthusiastic	Improvident = Sagittarius
Responsible	Dogmatic = Capricorn
Inventive	Eccentric = Aquarius
Imaginative	Hypersensitive = Pisces

Q2

(a) Pisces. The strange, exotic undersea world and its unfathomable mysteries attract the imaginative Fish personality.

(b) Taurus. The earth and all its products, both animal and vegetable, attract the solid Bull personality.

(c) Leo. The dramatic, colourful world of the stage and the sound of applause attract the lordly Lion personality.

(d) Sagittarius. The energetic, physical scene of the sporting world and the travel often associated with it attract the restless Centaur personality.

(e) Libra. The aesthetically oriented, beauty-creating world of cosmetics and the close contact with people attract the balanced Scales personality.

(f) Gemini. The fast-talking, verbal acrobatics of the world of sales and advertising plus the variety of scene associated with it attract the highly communicative Twins personality.

(g) Virgo. The painstaking attention to detail and creative handwork of the world of clothing attract the industrious Virgin personality.

(h) Scorpio. The love of danger and endless probing associated with all forms of detection attract the relentless Scorpio personality.

NB—The above occupations usually produce an instinctive attraction for the signs indicated. This does *not* mean all Pisceans will become divers for example. The entire chart of each individual must be considered in relation to aptitude for various types of work.

Q3

Assertion: putting the self across strongly; dislike of bossing by others or taking orders; inability to easily suppress own wishes to suit the needs of others in work and private life; expectation of 'getting own way' at all costs. Positivity and negativity do not define astrologically as these terms do in common speech:

Positivity (if stressed in a chart) promotes a marked urge towards self-expression in all life sectors. The self feels little need to repress its own desires and thus may find it hard to cooperate in the real sense with others. Pushes towards basic extroversion.

Negativity (if stressed in a chart) promotes a marked urge towards self-repression in all life sectors. The self experiences difficulty in pushing its own desires and thus may find itself imposed upon by others. Pulls towards basic introversion.

Q4

Majority of cardinal signs

(a) Inclined to take command of the situation; behave in an open, extroverted manner; state qualifications and experience forcefully to point of possible overstatement; give impression of desire for leadership opportunities (may suggest an egocentric approach).

(b) Inclined to expect intimates to fall into line with self's demands;

again to take control of decisions and future plans in personal affairs with others; give impression of somewhat wilful attitude; find it hard to give way to intimates on important matters.

Majority of mutable signs

(a) Inclined to let interview flow along, altering stance to suit situation; state qualifications and experience rather tentatively with understatement rather than overstatement likely; give impression of being willing to play 'second fiddle' (may suggest a wavering approach).

(b) Inclined to permit intimates to direct the self; display hesitation and often ambivalence in making decisions and future plans in personal affairs with others; give impression of being too 'bendable' in own attitudes; find it hard to demand 'a fair go' from intimates.

Q5

(a) Air. Like the element itself, predominantly air-type personalities blow hither and thither, avoiding 'heavy' scenes and thrusting life through the 'sieve' of the intellect. Their greatest asset is their innate ability to stand back and view themselves and the world in the round.

(b) Fire. Like the element itself, predominantly fire-type personalities crackle with energy, always leaping into situations and burning up themselves and sometimes others as well. Their greatest asset is their innate ability to bring enthusiasm and excitement to the world around them.

(c) Water. Like the element itself, predominantly water-type personalities swirl this way and that, driven by their ever-moving undercurrents of emotion. Their greatest asset is their innate ability to bring depths and intuitive understanding to the world around them.

(d) Earth. Like the element itself, predominantly earth-type personalities are dependably supportive, always in tune with the planet they live upon, predictable as its seasons. Their greatest asset is their innate ability to bring strength and solidarity to the world around them.

Q6
(a) Spend it to achieve the favourite scheme of the moment.
(b) Invest in land or houses where no security risk is likely.
(c) Apply it to current intellectual interest, later to the next current one and so on.
(d) Improve the home with a pool, antiques and fine furniture.
(e) Give a huge party for every imaginable friend/acquaintance.
(f) Invest it in the favoured occupation with view to cautious expansion.
(g) Buy or do anything that gives pleasure and people contact.
(h) Apply it to achieve power through money.
(i) Travel here, there and everywhere.
(j) Buy a major business and expand it.
(k) Sponsor inventors.
(l) Disappear to indulge the most cherished fantasy.

Q7
(a) Fire and water mixes are never easy to handle in relationships because the elements themselves are not really compatible. The fire person instinctively feels the water person will 'extinguish' them if given half a chance. The water person is always on guard against the fire person 'burning them up'.

With our example, the water type is the male and hence he could easily imagine his fire partner was insensitive to his moods, needs, basic sensitivity—that he was a sort of 'non-essential' to her life. This attitude could well bring on more moods, more water-type 'clamming up' hence exasperating the fire woman.

Her natural reaction would be to live her own life as much as possible, shutting him out and blaming him for his lack of obvious enthusiasm for whatever was turning her on at a given time.

Both fire and water represent extremism—the over-stress on passion (fire) and emotion (water). The resulting highs and lows here would be close to perpetual.
(b) This mix often leads to a somewhat sterile relationship. Air does not like the heavy stress on reality, the confining approach

of earth. On the other hand, earth feels literally 'dried out' by the winds of air, not knowing what point in the compass they are going to blow from next.

As the air person is the male in our example, he may secretly class his partner as being somewhat chore-oriented, overly practical and boring. Hence he would look for *his* kind of stimulation in the social scene—without her as much as possible. This approach is construed by earth as a blatant dereliction of duty, although in the end she could well set up a kind of 'windbreak' to keep him out of her life. Neither earth nor air are inclined to extremes so the relationship might continue for years with both offering the bare minimum to each other.

NB—In considering compatibility, the entire charts of both partners must be compared in detail. The clash between elemental stresses is only one factor.

Q8

(a) The positive stress would promote a more extroverted child, ready to experience the new scene without much hesitation. The cardinal stress would give the child the added impetus to show he 'could handle it', often with a desire to compete for attention with teachers and new classmates. The air stress would permit some intellectualization of the event, bring in as well a greater desire to integrate and 'socialize' with his peer group. Basically, a fairly easy child for an adult to introduce to the school environment.

(b) The negative stress would promote a more introverted, possibly tentative attitude towards the new experience. The mutable stress, however, allows enough adaptability to 'blend' into the class but without any wish to appear as a competitor or to assume a 'cocky' stance. The water stress would present some problem as water children are often somewhat fearful of being taken abruptly from the familiar, emotional links of the home to the unfamiliar world of strangers. Basically, a rather difficult child for an adult to introduce to the school environment. Comforting and reassurance could be vital.

Q9

This is a personal question and one's likes and dislikes in relation to others are of course representative of many more factors in the personal chart than the Sun sign alone. As a rough rule of thumb, you tend to find the most comfortable company with compatible elemental patterns. Water and earth often like each other, because water 'refreshes' earth on the one hand. Earth gives 'containment' to water.

The same rule generally applies to fire and air. Fire needs oxygen to keep burning; air likes the dazzle and crackling response of fire. If you have a special attraction towards or dislike of any particular sign, the reason for either reaction can always be traced in your own horoscope chart.

Sign	Symbol	Ruler	Category	Birth Cycle	Glyph
Aries	Ram	Mars	Positive Cardinal Fire	21 March-20 April	♈
Taurus	Bull	Venus	Negative Fixed Earth	21 April-21 May	♉
Gemini	Twins	Mercury	Positive Mutable Air	22 May-21 June	♊
Cancer	Crab	Moon	Negative Cardinal Water	22 June-23 July	♋
Leo	Lion	Sun	Positive Fixed Fire	24 July-23 Aug.	♌
Virgo	Virgin	Mercury	Positive Mutable Earth	24 Aug.-23 Sept.	♍

Sign	Symbol	Ruler	Category	Birth Cycle	Glyph
Libra	Scales	Venus	Positive Cardinal Air	24 Sept.-23 Oct.	♎
Scorpio	Scorpion	Pluto	Negative Fixed Water	24 Oct.-22 Nov.	♏
Sagittarius	Centaur	Jupiter	Positive Mutable Fire	23 Nov.-22 Dec.	♐
Capricorn	Goat	Saturn	Negative Cardinal Earth	23 Dec.-20 Jan.	♑
Aquarius	Water-Bearer	Uranus	Positive Fixed Air	21 Jan.-19 Feb.	♒
Pisces	Fish	Neptune	Negative Mutable Water	20 Feb.-20 Mar.	♓

Sign	Basic Interests	Negative Traits	Positive Traits
Aries	self-promotion; activity; leadership	impulse; pugnacity; quick temper; foolhardiness	courage; daring; enterprise; initiative
Taurus	possessions; property and land; physical comforts	obstinacy; stodginess; lack of drive; money-mindedness	strength; steadfastness; perseverance; dependability
Gemini	salesmanship of things and/or ideas; communication; literary matters	superficiality; over-inquisitiveness; lack of continuity	versatility; quick wits; mental agility
Cancer	home and family affairs; collecting valuable or sentimental items	touchiness; moods; over-protectiveness; crabby behaviour	sympathy; paternalism and mothering behaviour; sensitivity
Leo	rulership and command; stage, media, creative pursuits; organising others	patronizing manner; over-assurance; snobbery	generosity; sunniness; high-spirited behaviour
Virgo	work with precision and detail; health and hygiene; analysis of others	stand-offishness; over-criticism of self and others; perfectionism	modesty; discrimination; service to others

Sign	Basic Interests	Negative Traits	Positive Traits
Libra	the aesthetic ideal in art and environment working in people-oriented jobs; justice for all	inertia; indecisiveness; over-anxiety for peace	diplomacy; fairness; co-operation with others
Scorpio	Mysteries and the occult; tracking down problems; research	jealousy; brooding resentment; vengefulness	determination; penetrating intuition; bravery
Sagittarius	travel; philosophical pursuits; exploration	boastfulness; over-casual behaviour; carelessness	idealism; open-mindedness; enthusiasm
Capricorn	businesslike pursuits; social status; financial gain	meanness; social-climbing; materialism	orderliness; respect for tradition; prudence
Aquarius	humanitarian pursuits; the sciences; group activity	eccentricity; rebelliousness; fanaticism	originality; respect for freedom for self and others; friendliness
Pisces	spiritual matters; the arts; the sea	sloppiness; impracticality; escapism	kindness; imagination; refusal to judge others

2.

THE PLANETARY INFLUENCES

THE PLANETARY MEANINGS

Now you've got to closer grips with the twelve signs of the zodiac our next step along the rocky road to accurate astro-analysis takes us into tackling the planets. In these we include the Sun and Moon: although they are not planets in the strictly astronomical sense (and are sometimes called 'the lights' in textbooks) we regard them as such when examining their impact on human personality.

In order of personal significance, the celestial bodies are: the Sun, the Moon, Mercury, Venus, Mars, Jupiter, Saturn, Uranus, Neptune and Pluto. Each one represents a specific *principle* of human existence and consequently influences a specific *sector* of daily life.

You'll probably need to learn the planetary meanings off by heart at the outset of your study programme, but as you progress you'll discover you're gradually developing an instinctive understanding of their effects in every new horoscope chart you analyse.

We won't venture too far into the astronomical definitions of the planets, their history or the mythology surrounding their names, as some lengthy textbooks do. In any initial study course, this type of background information is not only unnecessary but often confusing and time-consuming as well. After you've learnt the techniques of astrological calculation and analysis set out in this course, you may want to dig deeper as an advanced student. If so, you'll find a list of recommended further reading at the end of the final section. Just a quick tip here, however. Should you decide to buy astrology books beforehand, always choose textbooks by authors whose qualifications are clearly stated therein. (There is still, sadly, much misinformed or over-generalized material being published about astrology by unqualified authors.) And never rely on Ascendant, Moon or other planetary tables printed in 'pop-type' paperbacks. These have to be averaged for the sake of brevity and can be quite incorrect, especially for individuals whose signs are near a cusp.

I have tried to avoid using jargon wherever possible and to explain each unfamiliar word as I go but if you're still at all uncertain, do buy a short encyclopaedia of astrology as soon as possible. Most bookshops stocking astrology texts have these in paperback for around £5.00.

By the way, you'll note as you work your way through the planetary meanings that the *first five*—Sun to Mars inclusive—apply most obviously to the *purely personal factors* in everybody's life. *The second five*—Jupiter to Pluto inclusive—apply more subtly to personality traits which are *harder to discern*. (That doesn't mean their effects are negligible!)

Just before we move further into this chapter we need to take a quick trip into the world of astronomy. As I stated earlier in this book, I have deliberately avoided discussing at length the links between the two sciences of astronomy and astrology because they are hard for beginners to grasp quickly and not within the province of a short work of this nature. (I know when *I* first tried to learn astrology from books back in the 1960s, those pages upon pages of sticky-looking diagrams and tables shook me to the core. I remember thinking: 'Ye Gods, you'd need an Honours degree in physics to come out on top of all this.')

However, if you wish later in your studies to examine areas where astrology and astronomy are inter-linked, some of the major reference works listed in Chapter 8 will supply all additional information. For now, we'll look at brief definitions of the zodiac and the ecliptic.

The zodiac and the ecliptic: what they are
Most astrological encyclopaedias give the definition of the zodiac as being a circle or belt of the heavens. The ecliptic is also defined

as a heavenly circle—a circle around which the Sun *appears* to move as it appears to journey round the earth. I emphasize 'appears' because in astronomical reality, the Earth in its orbit is actually revolving around the Sun.

This curious contradiction is rooted in the ancient past. When priests and scholars first began watching the heavens thousands of years ago, they saw—from their viewing point on Earth—the Sun rise over the eastern horizon at dawn and vanish below the western horizon at sunset. Thus, they naturally concluded, the Sun was travelling across the sky. It was not until the sixteenth century that the great astrologer/astronomer Kepler incontrovertibly established that the situation was the other way round. The Earth and not the Sun was really doing the moving.

Further, as you'll doubtless be aware, constellations of stars can be seen in the night sky with names which cover the twelve signs of the zodiac. Jeff Mayo in his classic text (see Book Reference List in Chapter 8) describes these particular constellations as 'the background' to the path of the ecliptic and adds that astrologers 'speak of the zodiac as being a belt of the sky which has the ecliptic as its centre'.

Do not despair if the foregoing sounds confusing. You don't have to worry about it in your astro-analysis work. We merely include it as a brief explanation of why in the following paragraph we state the Sun 'moves' or 'travels' through the twelve signs of the zodiac. All astrologers use these terms, but to be astronomically correct we should remind ourselves that such movement is actually only apparent.

Now, let's outline the specific influence of each of the celestial bodies in turn.

Sun
- Gives the light, warmth and energy without which no form of life on earth could continue to exist.
- Takes approximately thirty days to move through each sign of the zodiac, thus requiring one full year to travel through all twelve.
- Reveals how the *life-force* (or will) of any individual will manifest

itself according to the sign of the Sun occupies at birth, showing the true self, the natural mode of expression.
- Is tagged as a masculine 'planet', thus also representing significant masculine influences in each life, e.g., the father, male authority figures.
- Is depicted by the symbol ☉ in the horoscope chart.
- Rules (i.e., governs) the sign of Leo.

Moon
- Has no light of its own, merely reflecting solar brightness, and astronomically speaking is a satellite of the Earth.
- Moves the fastest of all the celestial bodies, travelling through the entire twelve signs of the zodiac in approximately twenty-eight days.
- Reveals how the *emotional behaviour* (or feelings) of any individual will manifest itself according to the sign the Moon occupies at birth—showing the instinctual capacity to respond, the childhood emotional conditioning.
- Is tagged as a feminine 'planet', thus also representing significant feminine influences in each life—e.g., the mother, female authority figures.
- Is depicted by this symbol ☽ in the horoscope chart.
- Rules (i.e., governs) the sign of Cancer.

Mercury
- Is the closest planet to the Sun (and the smallest) in the solar system and hence always occupies the same sign as the Sun or those immediately adjacent to that sign.
- Takes approximately eighty-eight days to travel through all twelve signs of the zodiac.
- Reveals how the *mentality* (or thinking) of any individual will manifest itself according to the sign Mercury occupies at birth—showing the natural mode of communication with others, the ability to verbalize needs.
- Is tagged as a neutral planet, thus absorbing the energies of any planet aspecting it.
- Is depicted by the symbol ☿ in the horoscope chart.

● Rules (i.e., governs) the signs of Gemini and Virgo.

Venus
● Is the second closest planet (excluding Earth) to the Sun after Mercury in the solar system.
● Takes approximately 224 days to travel through all twelve signs of the zodiac.
● Reveals how the *affectional needs* (or attractions) of any individual will manifest themselves according to the sign Venus occupies at birth, showing the capacity to attract and return love/affection, the urge to achieve satisfying relationships.
● Is tagged as a feminine planet, thus also representing appreciation of beauty and pleasures, inclination towards harmonious liaisons in each personality plus significant women other than the mother or mother figure.
● Is depicted by the symbol ♀ in the horoscope chart.
● Rules (i.e., governs) the signs of Taurus and Libra.

Mars
● Is the third closest planet (excluding Earth) to the Sun in the solar system.
● Takes approximately one year and 322 days to travel through all twelve signs of the zodiac.
● Reveals how the *sexual drive* (or animal energy) of any individual will manifest itself according to the sign Mars occupies at birth— showing the type of sexuality, the capacity to assert the self, the competitive urges.
● Is tagged as a masculine planet, thus also representing the degree of courage, capacity for physical endurance in each personality plus significant men other than the father or father figure.
● Is depicted by the symbol ♂ in the horoscope chart.
● Rules (i.e., governs) the sign of Aries and is co-ruler of Scorpio.

Jupiter
● Is the fourth closest planet (excluding Earth) to the Sun in the solar system.
● Takes approximately twelve years to travel through all twelve signs of the zodiac.

- Reveals how the *natural opportunism* (or ability to take chances) of any individual will manifest itself according to the sign Jupiter occupies at birth—showing the basic philosophy of life, the degree of tolerance and integrity.
- Is tagged as a masculine planet, thus also representing the development of occupational/professional skills, the aptitude for prospering in each personality.
- Is depicted by the symbol ♃ in the horoscope chart.
- Rules (i.e., governs) the sign of Sagittarius and is co-ruler of Pisces.

Saturn

- Is the fifth closest planet (excluding Earth) to the Sun in the solar system.
- Takes approximately 29½ years to travel through all twelve signs of the zodiac.
- Reveals how the *self-disciplinary capacity* (or ability to succeed) of any individual will manifest itself according to the sign Saturn occupies at birth—showing the willingness to be patient, accept limitations and learn from experience.
- Is tagged as a masculine planet, thus also representing the degree of self-control, the determination to overcome setbacks in each personality.
- Is depicted by the symbol ♄ in the horoscope chart.
- Rules (i.e., governs) the sign of Capricorn and is co-ruler of Aquarius.

Uranus

- Is the sixth closest planet (excluding Earth) to the Sun in the solar system.
- Takes approximately eighty-four years to travel through all twelve signs of the zodiac, hence can only reach them all in people who live to advanced old age.
- Reveals how the *independence drive* (or ability to initiate and deal with sudden changes) of any individual will manifest itself according to the sign Uranus occupies at birth, showing the potential for originality, the urge for personal freedom.

- Is tagged as a masculine planet, thus representing the degree of inventiveness, the outspokenness in each personality.
- Is depicted by the symbol ♅ in the horoscope chart.
- Rules (i.e., governs) the sign of Aquarius.

Neptune

- Is the seventh closest planet (excluding Earth) to the Sun in the solar system.
- Takes approximately 165 years to travel through all twelve signs of the zodiac, hence cannot reach them all in the human lifetime.
- Reveals how the *spiritual evolvement* (or ability to pursue ideals) of any individual will manifest itself according to the sign Neptune occupies at birth—showing the potential for inspiration, the power of imagination.
- Is tagged as a feminine planet, thus also representing the intrinsic subtlety, the willingness to renounce worldly gain in each personality.
- Is depicted by the symbol ♆ in the horoscope chart.
- Rules (i.e., governs) the sign of Pisces.

Pluto

- Is the most distant known planet from the Sun in the solar system. Takes approximately 248 years to travel through all twelve signs of the zodiac, hence cannot reach even half of them in the human lifetime.
- Reveals how the *self-regenerative power* (or ability to transform the self) of any individual will manifest itself according to the sign Pluto occupies at time of birth—showing the capacity to take extreme measures, to discard ruthlessly old or worthless concepts.
- Is tagged as a masculine planet, thus also representing the capacity to free the self, often forcefully, from ties or situations which seek to bind each personality.
- Is depicted by the symbol ♇ in the horoscope chart.
- Rules (i.e., governs) the sign of Scorpio.

You'll observe that the last three planets in the list—Uranus,

Neptune and Pluto—travel very slowly through the zodiac signs when you compare them to the first seven: e.g., the Moon finishes the complete circuit in twenty-eight days yet Pluto requires 248 years! This is why Uranus, Neptune and Pluto are termed 'generation planets'. Their lengthy sojourn in each sign stamps whole generation groups of human beings.

Every individual born in a particular *seven-year* period will show Uranus in the same sign in their charts. Every individual born in a particular *thirteen-year* period will show Neptune in the same sign in their charts. Every individual born in a particular *twelve to thirty-two-year* period will show Pluto in the same sign in their charts. (In Pluto's case, the period varies markedly because the planet's orbit is eccentric.)

When you reach the stage of calculating the horoscope chart and using the ephemeris (planetary position tables), you'll be able to check the planets' movements for yourself, noting when each one entered and left a given sign of the zodiac.

As far as setting up basic generation attitudes, Pluto is the most powerful influence. This planet is largely responsible for what is called 'the generation gap', or in plain terms, why parents and children diverge so far in mass consciousness (or 'gut reactions'). To illustrate: people born when Pluto was in Cancer (1914-39) are the parents of today's young and youngish adults, born when Pluto was in Leo (1939-57). How hard it is for those whose generation attitudes are subconsciously rooted in the home-and-country, honour-thy-parents and uphold-family-traditions territory of Cancer—to begin to comprehend their Pluto in Leo offspring or their tastes! All that wild crescendo of Leo vitality and excitement. The super-colourful gear, the roaring, pounding music beat, the 'I'll-do-it-my-way' stamp of the generation of the Lion.

This short sortie into generation planet theory is not a digression. Our next step will be to describe the specific influence of each of the first seven planets in our list through the twelve signs completely omitting Uranus, Neptune and Pluto. Why? Because in the astro-analysis of individual horoscope charts, the signs of these generation planets is of little significance. The houses of the horoscope they are located in *is*. But that matter belongs to the next section of the course.

Before we move on, here's quick-reference data on the planetary meanings to set them even more firmly in your mind.

Planetary meanings at a glance

Sun = Basic life attitudes	Core of being, ego drives, will-power
Moon = Instinctive responses	Source of emotions, hidden sensitivities, secret self.
Mercury = Communicative skills	Expression of needs, individual mentality, educational development.
Venus = Affectional behaviour	Reaction to love/affection, attraction to and for others, pleasures.
Mars = Sexual behaviour	Strength of sex drives, competitive energy, force of impulses.
Jupiter = Use of opportunities	Ability to expand and prosper, strength of natural optimism, personal growth.
Saturn = Degree of self-discipline	Ability to endure setbacks, acceptance of responsibilities, personal limitations.
Uranus = Degree of independence	Ability to make and cope with sudden changes in life-style, demand for personal freedom, inventiveness.
Neptune = Degree of spiritual development	Type of cultural expression, religious beliefs, intuitive powers.
Pluto = Capacity for self-regeneration	Strength of subconscious drives, inner transformation, hidden motivations.

THE PLANETS IN THE SIGNS OF THE ZODIAC

Now, we're ready to examine the effects of the Sun, the Moon, Mercury, Venus, Mars, Jupiter and Saturn in each of the twelve signs of the zodiac.

The basic definitions which follow need to be carefully digested and thought over—often! But do not regurgitate them willy-nilly when you approach a chart. Parrot-fashion learning or copying from any textbook or teacher is the telltale earmark of the amateur astrologer and produces a conglomeration of hopelessly conflicting personality traits and potentials.

As your expertise grows and your instinctive grasp of meanings develops, you'll discover, delightedly, your own interpretative style emerging from what once looked like a bottomless morass of detail. When it appears, don't try to clip its wings by following blindly my style or any other teacher's. But don't take off on your own flight too soon either. Remember, a little knowledge *is* a dangerous thing! It is all too easy to leap to quite wrong conclusions and hence give totally wrong advice on a chart. I well recall a novice astrologer who, when I recommended to her the views of a world leader on chart patterns, replied dismissively, 'I know better than he does!' Her own chart contained aspects implying both confused thinking and ill-founded intellectual arrogance—neither of which she was prepared to overcome. This was bad enough. But the damage such a person can do in counselling others is positively horrendous!

In each of the following definitions, you'll see both the pluses and minuses of each planet—how they can be expressed positively or negatively. Don't forget the Sun, the Moon and the planets all represent a specific *principle* of human existence.

The *sign* each one occupies at birth indicates the *manner* in which this principle will be expressed in your personality and everyone else's. The *house* placing of the planet (to be discussed in the next chapter) determines the *area* of your life where such influence will be most noticeable. The *aspects* to the planet (discussed in Chapter 4) will exert a further modifying effect.

When you have learnt how to combine all these factors

competently (and it's not as tough as it looks) you'll have begun to master the art of synthesis—of blending what first appear to be contradictory traits into a cohesive whole to provide a clear-cut picture of personality. But don't expect this picture to be one of perfect harmony. Human beings are awkward creatures and human nature is contrary! You do run across people who will be as forceful as a steam-roller in some situations, then act like the original shrinking violet in others!

Basic nature as shown by Sun sign

Sun in Aries: ☉ ♈
This makes your basic nature that of an ardent, eager, enthusiastic individual, whose reaction to life is fundamentally energetic and impulsive. Your basic approach is frank, direct and forceful.

Aries also predisposes towards egotism, lack of deep understanding of the feelings of others and marked impatience. Others may feel that your mistakes are too easily forgotten and you never look before you leap.

Sun in Taurus: ☉ ♉
This makes your basic nature that of a self-reliant, stable, persistent individual, who always proceeds constructively, with a careful eye on the final outcome of words or actions. Your basic approach is highly practical, slow but sure, and very determined.

Taurus also predisposes towards marked inflexibility, secretiveness, and overemphasis on material gain. Others may find your tendency to sudden, blind anger when thwarted hard to accept.

Sun in Gemini: ☉ ♊
This makes your basic nature that of a bright, talkative, versatile individual, who enjoys constant contact with others and can easily handle two totally different jobs at once. Your basic approach is cool, inquisitive and lively.

Gemini also predisposes towards independability, lack of concentration and heartlessness. Others may find your 'always on the go' attitude agitating and your tendency to become bored with routine very annoying.

Sun in Cancer: ☉ ♋
This makes your basic nature that of an impressionable, reserved and emotional individual whose reaction to life is fundamentally family-oriented and conventional. Your basic approach is tenacious and intuitive.

Cancer also predisposes towards moodiness, over-impressionability and a tendency to look on the gloomy side of things. Others may feel you are somewhat of a 'wet blanket' at times.

Sun in Leo: ☉ ♌
This makes your basic nature that of a dignified, generous, strong-willed individual whose reaction to life is both forceful and autocratic. Your basic approach is commanding and broad-minded.

Leo also disposes towards laziness, personal vanity and great susceptibility to flattery. Others may think you too extravagant, forthright and self-assertive.

Sun in Virgo: ☉ ♍
This makes your basic nature that of a self-effacing, sensible, aloof person who operates best in a working environment and does not much enjoy social life. Your basic approach is practical and critical.

Virgo also predisposes towards fault-finding and over-attention to detail. Others may regard you as fussy, cold and unresponsive.

Sun in Libra: ☉ ♎
This makes your basic nature that of an easy-going, objective individual, who does not take sides and is generally regarded as just and impartial. Your basic approach is pleasant and fair-minded.

Libra also predisposes towards over-objectivity and inconsistency, plus self-centred interests. Others may consider you too frivolous and shallow.

Sun in Scorpio: ☉ ♏
This makes your basic nature that of a taciturn, resourceful individual, who can never accept compromise or defeat. Your basic approach is penetrating, perceptive and wary.

Scorpio also predisposes towards envy, possessiveness and

sarcasm. Others may find your self-control too heavy and your silences impenetrable.

Sun in Sagittarius: ☉ ♐

This makes your basic nature that of a friendly, philosophical, freedom-loving individual who is always looking for new adventures and wider horizons. Your basic approach is frank, direct and sincere.

Sagittarius also predisposes towards carelessness, extravagance and exaggeration. Others may find your tendency to sulk and lack of attention to detail irritating.

Sun in Capricorn: ☉ ♑

This makes your basic nature that of a conservative and success-oriented individual whose reaction to life is fundamentally serious and conventional. Your basic approach is cautious and methodical.

Capricorn also predisposes towards lack of enthusiasm, periods of melancholy and depression. Others may regard you as uninspiring, too work-oriented and somewhat joyless.

Sun in Aquarius: ☉ ♒

This makes your basic nature that of an idealistic, original and strongly humanitarian individual, who puts intense energy into unorthodox, even revolutionary ideas. Your basic approach is friendly, but curiously impersonal.

Aquarius also predisposes towards eccentricity, fanatically unconventional attitudes and erratic thinking. Others may regard you as lacking in solidarity of principle, too detached and patronising.

Sun in Pisces: ☉ ♓

This makes your basic nature that of a romantic, gentle individual, who is rather unworldly and very idealistic due to your innate urge to trust everybody. Your basic approach is sympathetic, sensitive and compassionate.

Pisces also predisposes towards vagueness, moodiness and periods of marked self-doubt. Others may regard you as too timid and prone to fruitless daydreaming.

Emotional potential as shown by Moon sign

Moon in Aries: ☽ ♈
This implies that your responses to emotional stimuli are quick, spontaneous and direct. At the time of stimulation, they are keen and intense but not lasting, thus implying lack of real depth.

Moon in Taurus: ☽ ♉
This implies that your responses to emotional stimuli are steady, gentle, and closely linked to a liking for all the good things of the Earth. Once you make up your mind on an emotional issue, you rarely change it.

Moon in Gemini: ☽ ♊
This implies that your responses to emotional stimuli are positive, restless and extremely changeable. There is a lifelong desire for variety in associations, which also makes you fickle, facile and often too versatile.

Moon in Cancer: ☽ ♋
This implies that your responses to emotional stimuli are very deep and oriented towards domestic issues. Powerful intuitions guide behaviour, providing an apparent self-assurance that is not easily understood by intimates.

Moon in Leo: ☽ ♌
This implies that your responses to emotional stimuli are positive, dramatic and even theatrical. This urge to be the centre of attraction also makes you proud and very easily offended if others do not respond to you in the way you desire.

Moon in Virgo: ☽ ♍
This implies that your responses to emotional stimuli are directed more towards service to others rather than demonstrative displays. The acuity of impressions through both the mind and senses is greatly increased but partly concealed by coolness.

Moon in Libra: ☽ ♎
This implies that your responses to emotional stimuli exhibit a strong sensitivity to the attitudes and reactions of others, particularly

the marriage partner. The emotional dependence on those close to you is too strong so that you are often too easily influenced by intimates.

Moon in Scorpio: ☽ ♏
This implies that your responses to emotional stimuli are proud, self-willed and obsessive. There is an inclination to demand too much from intimates and give insufficient understanding in return.

Moon in Sagittarius: ☽ ♐
This implies that your responses to emotional stimuli exhibit marked adaptability so that you find it relatively easy to achieve workable relationships with others. But with this approach comes an unquenchable desire for freedom and independence.

Moon in Capricorn: ☽ ♑
This implies that your responses to emotional stimuli are conservative, distrustful and very conventional. There is a need to dissolve this rigidity by making a greater effort to understand others and to avoid too much adherence to parental precepts.

Moon in Aquarius: ☽ ♒
This implies that your responses to emotional stimuli are pleasant and friendly yet mask a very marked inner coolness. Your feelings tend to be cramped and restricted by thinking about them instead of acting upon them.

Moon in Pisces: ☽ ♓
This implies that your responses to emotional stimuli are deeply romantic, sympathetic and voluble. Super-sensitivity to the attitudes of others and your environment generally causes you to be very vulnerable.

Mental potential as shown by Mercury sign

Mercury in Aries: ☿ ♈
This indicates that your type of mind is positive, impetuous and impulsive. New ideas are picked up eagerly and reactions to mental impressions are trigger-quick. There is, however, a clear need to develop better concentration.

Mercury in Taurus: ☿ ♉
This indicates that your type of mind is conservative and more is learned from travel and experience than from textbooks. However, it is essential to avoid rigidity or stubbornness in all mental activities.

Mercury in Gemini: ☿ ♊
This indicates that your type of mind is quick and bright, sometimes too much so. All thought activity is restless and exceptionally versatile. There is a need to develop greater steadiness and concentration of mental effort.

Mercury in Cancer: ☿ ♋
This indicates that your type of mind is so emotionally slanted and receptive to the ideas of others that it can lose its clarity in a sea of feelings. The mind is passive, but often psychic and learns better through listening to others rather than study.

Mercury in Leo: ☿ ♌
This indicates that your type of mind exhibits a strong will and a firm fixity of purpose—once a clear objective has been chosen. Dislike of serious mental activity must be overcome to achieve your full potential.

Mercury in Virgo: ☿ ♍
This indicates that your type of mind is logical, practical and governed by a strong infusion of common sense. Problems are a disinclination to concentrate long enough to master subjects and a tendency to over-analyse.

Mercury in Libra: ☿ ♎
This indicates that your type of mind is sensitive, balanced and positive on the surface, but often indecisive and vacillating underneath. Problem is this gives a factual, overly 'masculine' positivity to methods of thought—even in females.

Mercury in Scorpio: ☿ ♏
This indicates that your type of mind is quick and perceptive so that it is very easy to see the flaws or weaknesses in other people's arguments. Resistance shows when any attempt is made to pin

you down to a clear statement of intention.

Mercury in Sagittarius: ☿ ♐
This indicates that your type of mind is quick and keen but lacks direction. You tackle mental work willingly and capably but often lack the application to see it through to the finish.

Mercury in Capricorn: ☿ ♑
This indicates that your type of mind is serious and earnest exhibiting a consequent lack of humour and 'heavy' attitudes. Intolerance and pessimism are matters to watch, as is a tendency to be overly materialistic.

Mercury in Aquarius: ☿ ♒
This indicates that your type of mind is resourceful, balanced and capable of good judgement. Connections with group activities or large organizations are enjoyed. Thought patterns slant towards humane, modernistic attitudes.

Mercury in Pisces: ☿ ♓
This indicates that your type of mind is poetic, impressionable and innately refined. You are likely to be too much influenced in your thinking by those close to you, which creates vagueness and lack of determination.

Love potential as shown by Venus sign

Venus in Aries: ♀ ♈
This sets up passionate, impetuous reactions to love and affection. There is a risk of being inconsiderate to those loved without even realizing it due to overstress on impulse.

Venus in Taurus: ♀ ♉
This sets up a longing for constant, lasting forms of love and affection. You can be possessive towards those close to you but in a passive rather than interfering manner.

Venus in Gemini: ♀ ♊
This sets up reactions to love and affection that are light, charming and expressive. Variety and intellectual stimulation are so

constantly desired, it is almost impossible for you to remain constant to one individual.

Venus in Cancer: ♀ ♋
This sets up a deep sentimentality towards all forms of love and affection rather than ardent displays of either. There is too much need for security together with a degree of over-dependency on the family group.

Venus in Leo: ♀ ♌
This sets up ardent, fixed reactions to love and affection, coupled with great love of life. Marked loyalty to the love partner is present but there is always a wish for the sort of spouse who can be 'shown off'.

Venus in Virgo: ♀ ♍
This sets up an inclination to over-analyse feelings of love and affection, creating often sharp criticism of those loved. This is a danger as it causes love partners to feel constantly self-conscious as well as inhibited in the expression of affection.

Venus in Libra: ♀ ♎
This sets up responses to love and affection that are an unusual mixture of intellectual appreciation and romantic behaviour. You, yourself, display an inborn pleasantness and high standards of conduct but rely too much on outward appearances.

Venus in Scorpio: ♀ ♏
This sets up reactions to love and affection that are deep, intense and undeviating. You tend to expect that all the giving in any relationship should come from the other party.

Venus in Sagittarius: ♀ ♐
This sets up reactions to love and affection that are demonstrative, friendly and 'breezy'. But it also makes for unreliability in love due to the fact that the eyes are always on greener fields and new partners.

Venus in Capricorn: ♀ ♑
This sets up a great need for security in love and affection coupled

with a deep fear of overt or public displays. This can be misunderstood, for your love nature is far from cold and you can be very loving and loyal in private.

Venus in Aquarius: ♀ ♒
This sets up reactions to love and affection that are cool, calm and collected. As a result, you always appear righteous, ethical and correct with intimates, but may often give the impression of some lack of deep response.

Venus in Pisces: ♀ ♓
This sets up reactions to love and affection that are gentle, understanding and highly compassionate. Too much romanticism and capacity for self-sacrifice tempt others to impose upon you.

Sex potential as shown by Mars sign

Mars in Aries: ♂ ♈
This indicates that your responses to sexual stimuli are ardent, energetic and enthusiastic. This overstress on self-assertion infers real consideration of the moods or feelings of the lover are treated lightly (at best), ignored (at worst).

Mars in Taurus: ♂ ♉
This indicates that your responses to sexual stimuli are strong and sensual in an earthy way, but slow to arouse. There is marked danger of sexual jealousy and possessiveness, both of which need to be curbed.

Mars in Gemini: ♂ ♊
This indicates that your responses to sexual stimuli are light, bright and lively, but not intense. Much more energy is directed towards talk than action. The search for new and entertaining partners is lifelong.

Mars in Cancer: ♂ ♋
This indicates that your responses to sexual stimuli are sympathetic, sensitive and intuitive, but not aggressive. Also indicates a strong desire to build a happy, well-run domestic environment, yet at the same time there is recurring strife therein.

Mars in Leo: ♂ ♌
This indicates that your responses to sexual stimuli are positive, passionate and enthusiastic. There is a need to watch for and curb both jealousy and demanding behaviour as both militate against satisfying, reciprocal relationships.

Mars in Virgo: ♂ ♍
This indicates that your responses to sexual stimuli are hard to please and 'perfectionist', coupled with a practical, down-to-earth physical reaction. For these reasons, there is a continuing risk of misunderstandings, especially if the sex partner is either ardent or sensual.

Mars in Libra: ♂ ♎
This indicates that your responses to sexual stimuli are aimed towards establishing relationships where you will be noticed and admired. There is a strong desire for marriage, although unions are often limited by an overstrong need for co-operation from intimates.

Mars in Scorpio: ♀ ♏
This indicates that your responses to sexual stimuli are intense and passionate, the 'all-or-nothing-at-all' approach. Possessiveness and jealousy are the twin dangers to watch for, and both are fuelled by stubbornness, strong will and personal pride.

Mars in Sagittarius: ♀ ♐
This indicates that your responses to sexual stimuli are impulsive, energetic and direct. Because of the uninhibited flow of physical energy, you can be too frank and at times inconsiderate of your partner.

Mars in Capricorn: ♀ ♑
This indicates that your responses to sexual stimuli are aimed towards the attainment of material objectives rather than the expression of physical desires. This checks and restrains animal energies so that it is very hard to 'let yourself go'.

Mars in Aquarius: ♀ ♒
This indicates that your responses to sexual stimuli are

unconventional, rebellious and independent. This dispassionate, impersonal approach to sex makes total physical abandonment virtually impossible for you.

Mars in Pisces: ♀ ✕
This indicates that your responses to sexual stimuli are sensitive, highly romantic and over-impressionable. There is a deceptively passive behaviour in sexual confrontations, which masks a deeply felt sense of restlessness and indecision.

Opportunity potential as shown by Jupiter sign

Jupiter in Aries: ♃ ✕
This Jupiter indicates that opportunities will come to you throughout life as a result of enterprise and energy, coupled with a strong sense of self-esteem. Leadership qualities are well developed as are love of freedom and independence. But check over-expansive behaviour.

Jupiter in Taurus: ♃ ♉
This indicates that opportunities will come to you throughout life as a result of your innate capacity to attract money and material possessions. Money is of paramount importance to you so there is a need to watch for an overly materialistic attitude.

Jupiter in Gemini: ♃ ✕
This indicates that opportunities will come to you throughout life as a result of your ability to 'sell' your ideas to others. Chances of overseas travel occur on a number of occasions during your lifetime. Concentrate efforts more cohesively and check rash statements.

Jupiter in Cancer: ♃ ♋
This indicates that opportunities will come to you throughout life as a result of your care for and genuine interest in others, plus a kindly approach. You should acquire both cash and property, provided security-consciousness is not allowed to dominate.

Jupiter in Leo: ♃ ♌
This indicates that opportunities will come to you throughout life

as a result of your physical vitality, courage and loyalty. Also stimulates marked personal dignity which makes it easier for you to impress others. This urge to 'show off' does need to be somewhat curbed.

Jupiter in Virgo: ♃ ♍

This indicates that opportunities will come to you throughout life as a result of your willingness to render practical service to others. However, you demand extraordinary integrity of detail and often exhibit a moralistic concern for perfection which annoys colleagues.

Jupiter in Libra: ♃ ♎

This indicates that opportunities will come to you throughout life as a result of your ability to act justly, impartially and kindly towards others. Watch somewhat vacillating behaviour in grasping chances and indecisive behaviour.

Jupiter in Scorpio: ♃ ♏

This indicates that opportunities will come to you throughout life as a result of your capacity for shrewd, critical judgement of people and situations. You are inclined to be very intense and uncompromising. Check this attitude as it can create bitter enemies!

Jupiter in Sagittarius: ♃ ♐

This indicates that opportunities will come to you throughout life as a result of your capacity for optimistic, outgoing behaviour, making you the type with whom others will work willingly. You have an innate instinct to take the main chance, but check opportunistic behaviour.

Jupiter in Capricorn: ♃ ♑

This indicates that opportunities will come to you throughout life as a result of your innate capacity to work conscientiously and reliably. There is, however, a need to let yourself 'think bigger' and relax the tendency towards over-cautiousness which restricts your potential.

Jupiter in Aquarius: ♃ ♒

This indicates that opportunities will come to you throughout life as a result of your innate capacity to take a broad, humanitarian view and idealistic motivation. There is a need, however, to watch impractical idealism which spreads scope of interest beyond the natal abilities.

Jupiter in Pisces: ♃ ✕
This indicates that opportunities will come to you throughout life as a result of your natural desire to help others—quietly, unobtrusively, without expectation of reward. Still, rewards do come in the form of praise and favours—provided you do not allow yourself to be imposed upon.

Achievement potential as shown by Saturn sign

Saturn in Aries: ♄ ♈
This suggests achievement of ambitions as a result of physical energy, teamed with reasoning powers. The need is to overcome suspicion and distrust of the motives of others, which may be linked with a deep-rooted father complex.

Saturn in Taurus: ♄ ♉
This suggests achievement of ambitions as a result of stubborn, persistent pursuit. You would not be easily diverted from your prime objective which is clearly the attainment of a high standard of living. Check envy of those better off, which needs to be controlled.

Saturn in Gemini: ♄ ♊
This suggests achievement of ambitions as a result of your enquiring mind and capacity to perceive the inner meaning of life. But it does incline towards negativism, nerve strain and physical tension. It is thus essential to develop a positive, optimistic faith in yourself.

Saturn in Cancer: ♄ ♋
This suggests achievement of ambitions as a result of acceptance of family responsibilities. Your attachment to material possessions limits your achievements by creating hypersensitivity and defensiveness. This touchiness inhibits success.

Saturn in Leo: ♄ ♌
This suggests achievement of ambitions as a result of drive towards status and importance, coupled with a compulsion to rule your

own life and the lives of those close to you. If self-discipline is not imposed, these can create too much egotism and desire for power.

Saturn in Virgo: ♄ ♍

This suggests achievement of ambitions as a result of work involving minute attention to detail. Also stimulates needless worrying and fits of depression when faced by temporary setbacks. Likely to be overly critical with colleagues or associates.

Saturn in Libra: ♄ ♎

This suggests achievement of ambitions as a result of co-operation with others, together with the establishment of lasting relationships through patience, responsibility and humility. Gives good judgement in assessing objectives, but 'hard-line' reactions need to be watched.

Saturn in Scorpio: ♄ ♏

This suggests achievement of ambitions as a result of innate shrewdness and resourcefulness. There is always an intense drive for personal power based on emotional, physical and mental strengths. Often produces disconcerting moods where you withdraw into yourself.

Saturn in Sagittarius: ♄ ♐

This suggests achievement of ambitions as a result of attraction to higher education in various forms. You have (a perhaps unrealized) wish to be regarded as an authority in your chosen field of intellectual interest, but check a deep-seated fear of disapproval or censure.

Saturn in Capricorn: ♄ ♑

This suggests achievement of ambitions as a result of acquisition of power and personal prestige. If the other parts of life are neglected as a result of the success drive, then loneliness, feelings of frustration and isolation result. The sense of duty and responsibility is overstressed.

Saturn in Aquarius: ♄ ♒

This suggests achievement of ambitions as a result of group effort and boosts an impersonal scientific approach to problems. The main danger is too much intellectual pride which can give the impression of coldness.

Saturn in Pisces: ♄ ⧓
This suggests achievement of ambitions as a result of introspection, compassion and the capacity to identify very personally with other people's difficulties. A high degree of self-consciousness stems in part from subconscious fears, so it is vital to let go of the past.

Before you conclude your study of the planets, give yourself a simple test. Compare the sign data you learned in Chapter 1 with the planetary data you've just learned in this chapter. Check if you can pick up the correlation between signs and planets.

To illustrate: you'll recall the plus traits of Pisces promote sympathy and kindness towards others. You'll recall the planet Jupiter shows how opportunities in life are handled. Result? Jupiter occupying the sign of Pisces in any natal chart implies opportunities of benefit to the self will arise from acts of help or good turns to those in need.

Now, try some of the others by yourself and gauge how your feel for interpretation is progressing.

TEST EXERCISES

1. In the same way as the twelve signs of the zodiac, the ten planets can be expressed in either *plus* or *minus* manner. Select the two nouns in the list below which, in your opinion, pinpoint the *plus* and *minus* qualities of each planet's influence, excluding in this instance, the Sun.

changefulness	pugnacity
expansion	perversity
elimination	artfulness
aspiration	irrationality
energy	pacification
adroitness	opportunism
magnetism	subversion
artistry	destruction
spirituality	depression

2. The Moon-Venus-Mars mix represents the often conflicting needs of each individual in the areas of emotional response and affectional and sexual drives. Describe briefly the likely love behaviour of a male whose chart showed:
   (a) Moon in Capricorn
      Venus in Virgo
      Mars in Virgo
   (b) Moon in Pisces
      Venus in Aquarius
      Mars in Aries
   (c) If the above planetary mixes appeared in a female chart, what differences, if any, would you expect?

3. American psychologist/astrologer Noel Tyl, describing the interaction of the Sun-Moon blend in individual charts, calls the Moon 'the reigning need' of each personality. What effect would you consider the Moon's influence over Sun sign behaviour to produce in the following birth patterns:
   (a) Sun in Libra and Moon in Aquarius
   (b) Sun in Aries and Moon in Cancer
   (c) Sun in Sagittarius and Moon in Gemini
   (d) Sun in Scorpio and Moon in Virgo

4. State the approach to mental effort, direction of intellectual interests and type of ambitions in individuals with:
   (a) Mercury in Aries and Saturn in Leo
   (b) Mercury in Libra and Saturn in Libra
   (c) Mercury in Taurus and Saturn in Sagittarius
   (d) Mercury in Gemini and Saturn in Virgo

5. American author Robert Worth contends that the signs which Venus and Mars occupy in a chart reveal whether or not such a person can or cannot hurt others—even unwittingly—in close love or family relationships. Consider the following planetary pairs and state which falls into the 'can hurt' and 'can't hurt' categories:
   (a) Venus in Cancer and Mars in Pisces
   (b) Venus in Aquarius and Mars in Capricorn
   (c) Venus in Leo and Mars in Scorpio
   (d) Venus in Gemini and Mars in Sagittarius

6. Prince Charles and Princess Diana are undoubtedly the most famous married couple of the 1980s. If you were asked to counsel them astrologically on points of clash and compatibility, what clues about their union would you gather from the following planetary positions?

Prince Charles		Princess Diana	
Sun	Scorpio	Sun	Cancer
Moon	Taurus (but very close to cusp of Aries)	Moon	Aquarius
		Mercury	Cancer
		Venus	Taurus
Mercury	Scorpio	Mars	Virgo (but very close to cusp of Leo)
Venus	Libra		
Mars	Sagittarius		

7. Authors writing on medical astrology assign specific roles to the planets in affecting overall health. Below are the titles given to each planet in this regard. State which planet you think belongs to which title:

the Inflamer; the Sustainer; the Relaxer; the Vitalizer; the Dissolver; the Depriver; the Electrifier; the Transmitter; the Transformer; the Protector.

8. Here follow 'capsule' comments on certain planets in certain signs. Note the sign and planet you think belongs to each comment.

(a) 'In emotional liaisons, likely to be over-assertive, but passionate—quick-tempered if intentions are misunderstood.'

(b) 'Much attracted to the good life and to partners who share this attitude—but can be possessive of intimates.'

(c) 'Very practical and realistic in thinking and expression of opinion—but often dogmatic and narrow in viewpoint.'

(d) 'Very intense desires, loyal, strong—but inclined to demand too much in sexual involvements.'

(e) 'Notably patient and reasonably controlled in pursuit of life aims—but tends to isolate the self from others.'

(f) 'Likely to grasp all types of opportunities with alacrity, and versatile in applying talents towards advancement—but often appears overly clever and slick.'

9. Matters of love, sex and family are probably the main areas in which advice is sought from the practising astrologer today. If one party's planetary positions appeared markedly disharmonious to the other party's showing strong divergence in life goals, attitude to love, approach to children, use of finances, how would you advise such a couple:
   (a) Tell them to cut their losses and quit?
   (b) Indicate the possible clash-points and suggest how these can be overcome.
   (c) Sit on the fence and stick to generalized comments?
   (d) Attempt to play the role of an impartial arbitrator?

10. Set out below in a deliberately jumbled order are the glyphs (shorthand symbols) of the signs and planets. Write out these glyphs in your own hand, teaming each planet with the sign it rules and placing the signs in their natural order around the wheel of the horoscope.

   1. ♒ ♃   2. ♉ ♐   3. ♌ ☽   4. ♀ ♓
   5. ♅ ♒   6. ♆ ♏   7. ♍ ♇   8. ♂ ♋
   9. ☉ ♈   10. ♄ ☿   11. ♄ ♎   12. ♓ ♅

MODEL ANSWERS

Note
The model answers given in the following pages are offered in fairly brief outline as guidance to each test participant. Your own answers do not have to be exactly the same to be marked as correct. Original thinking is always rewarded, provided that your ideas show you have learned and understood the basic tenets of astrological theory.

Q1

Pluses	*Minuses*
Changefulness	Irrationality = Moon
Adroitness	Artfulness = Mercury
Artistry	Pacification = Venus
Energy	Pugnacity = Mars

Expansion..............................Opportunism = Jupiter
Aspiration.............................Depression = Saturn
Magnetism...........................Perversity = Uranus
Spirituality ....Subversion = Neptune
Elimination ....Destruction = Pluto

These nouns represent attitudes generated by the planet concerned but, as ever, aspects, signs, house positions indicate how strong each influence will be in either positive or negative expression in behaviour.

Q2

(a) Emotionally, a very markedly earthy type who looks for practical results in relationships. Can be sensual but rarely in a romantic or demonstrative manner. Inclination towards doubt and cynicism as to motivations of partners, whether potential or existing. Highly goal-oriented, even in love and sex. Possibly ruthless in assessment of those loved. Self-abandonment in love is virtually impossible.

Both sexes exhibit these behavioural patterns. But in females, due to conditioning and role of sexes, greater effort would be expended to disguise what is basically a perfectionist, aloof reaction.

Nevertheless, the cohesive earth blend is often supportive and without shocks or surprises. Feeling is shown through help to those loved in form of acts of service or financial assistance.

(b) Emotionally quite the opposite to (a). Very contrary, interesting but unpredictable set of behavioural responses. Veers around from fantasy to intellectuality to wild passion in intimate relationships. Partners, potential or existing, need to understand sudden swings in mood or demand. Sometimes unbridled romanticism collides with impersonal friendliness (Pisces+Aquarius) then back to ardour that can be mind-bogglingly urgent (Aries). Both sexes exhibit these behavioural patterns. But, in females, again due to conditioning and role of sexes, some attempt would probably be made to appear more amenable in early stages of relationships.

The contrary blends are not supportive. Partners are expected

to understand and tune in to the governing mood of the
moment.

Q3

(a) This is a trine, promoting easier interaction between will (Sun)
and emotions (Moon)—regardless of orb. Sometimes the tough,
superior attitudes of Aquarius can add greater definition and
backbone to Libran indecision. Good taste and air of good
breeding prevent the eccentricity of Aquarius from shocking
others.

(b) This is a square, promoting a baulking interaction between
will (Sun) and emotions (Moon)—regardless of orb. The
inherent swagger of Aries is somewhat undermined by Cancer's
supersensitivity. Typical Cancer demands for home/children
collide with Aries drive and ambition to show self off as a tireless
leader. Sometimes, the self is not sure precisely what it wants
or just where it's going.

(c) This is an opposition, promoting clash of demand between
will (Sun) and emotions (Moon)—regardless of orb. Both
Sagittarius and Gemini become bored easily, so adventure and
change oust commonsense or pursuit of realistic goals. The
inherent optimism and capacity to grasp opportunities of
Sagittarius finds no solid anchor in Gemini so rewards sought
in life can be too diverse.

(d) This is a sextile, promoting fairly comfortable interchange
between will (Sun) and emotions (Moon)—regardless of orb.
The inherent emotionalism and intuition of Scorpio is aided
by the sharpness of perception shown by Virgo. Although both
are introverted signs, Scorpio and Virgo work together to create
a strong personal code of ethics, which, when called upon,
will be stated uncategorically.

Note: Remember, as we'll see later in this course, the influence
of the Ascendant must also be blended with the above set of
responses.

Q4

(a) Bright, fast thinker with vigorous, unequivocal and direct powers of communication. Ambitions are fiery too, so mentality is applied to achieve admiration, applause and seek dramatic outlets. This is a trine. Causes no problem for its owner.

(b) Very intellectual type with balanced, aesthetically-oriented mentality. Ambitions are markedly intellectual too, but never inclined to extremes and modified by instinctive awareness of others' needs, hence promoting co-operation. This is a conjunction. Comfortable link for its owner.

(c) Slow, practical thinker, capable of more patient assessment of ideas. Learns best from experience instead of books. Ambitions are very idealistic, passionately felt and the capacity to inspire others is marked. This is a quincunx. May cause annoying divergence of needs for its owner.

(d) Versatile, quick mind, highly verbal communicator. Capable of handling many intellectual pursuits at once. Ambitions are much more down-to-earth, forcing increased seriousness in pursuit of goals. This is a square. May cause infuriating tension to its owner.

Note: Remember, the Sun and Jupiter also affect the achievement of ambitions and the manner in which mental skills are applied.

Q5

(a) 'Can't hurt'. This is a trine. Predictable, without tension. Feels no need to strike out at intimates.

(b) 'Can hurt'. This is a semi-sextile. Needs vary too widely, thus hard to satisfy. Disappointment may cause coldness to intimates.

(c) 'Can hurt'. This is a square. Affectional and sexual demands are pushed in separate directions. Frustration may cause outbursts against intimates.

(d) 'Can't hurt'. This is an opposition, but not a damaging one. Quickly perceptive, not really demanding. As long as intimates do not attempt to restrict, no desire to attack exists.

Q6

Both Charles and Diana show strong water stress, promoting

emotionalism, intuition and receptivity to needs of others. Two Mercurys in trine suggest easier communication. Two Suns in trine suggest more compatible pursuit of life goals.

But marked and potentially destructive clashes also exist. Charles' Sun (his masculinity) collides with Diana's Moon (her femininity). His old-fashioned, 'heavy' male attitudes find no response from her ultra-modern, 'new-wave woman' female attitudes. Her underlying unconventionalism and contempt for formalities would disturb him. She would feel the heavy weight of unwanted protocol.

Some problems with sexual expression here too. His Mars desires freedom and variety. Her Mars switches from critical aloofness to demand for worshipping admiration.

The two Venuses are not easy either. Charles can intellectualize affection, seeking only peace and harmony. Diana is possessive in affection, very physical.

Above is, of course, only a brief outline of the relationship between this couple. Many other factors have to be examined and advised upon. Nevertheless, the prognosis for this union is far from excellent. Both will have to exert a great deal of understanding and restraint if their marriage is to continue satisfactorily. Press comment has already shown problems in life sectors set out above.

Q7

The Inflamer	Mars
The Vitalizer	Sun
The Transmitter	Mercury
The Transformer	Pluto
The Dissolver	Neptune
The Electrifier	Uranus
The Relaxer	Venus
The Depriver	Saturn
The Protector	Jupiter
The Sustainer	Moon

Note: If interested in the types of diseases and ailments suggested by specific planets, see Dr H. L. Cornell's *Encyclopaedia of Medical Astrology.*

Q8

(a) Moon in Aries
(b) Venus in Taurus
(c) Mercury in Capricorn
(d) Mars in Scorpio
(e) Saturn in Libra
(f) Jupiter in Gemini

Q9

In view of all psychologist/astrologers, counselling must be offered in a *positive* manner. This means accentuating the assets of each personality to promote the kind of right thinking that will contribute to avoiding or mitigating problem areas.

Approaches (a) and (c) are both contrary to this goal in counselling. One must never dictate a course of action to clients: the decisions must remain theirs. Equally, to be non-committal is unhelpful, implying the counsellor is afraid of making critical statements that will throw light on problem areas.

Approach (d) has some virtue if two clients refuse to see their relationship dispassionately.

Approach (b) is, generally, the best, provided compatible pointers have been well-stressed first. Clash-points, often unrealized or unstated, or both, can magnify over years to destroy a relationship, which if worked upon willingly, would have survived and offered valuable learning to both partners.

Q10

1. ♈ ♂	2. ♉ ♀	3. ♓ ☿	4. ♋ ☽
5. ♌ ☉	6. ♍ ☿	7. ♎ ♀	8. ♏ ♇
9. ♐ ♃	10. ♑ ♄	11. ♒ ♅	12. ♓ ♆

3.

THE HOUSES
OF THE HOROSCOPE

THE HOUSES: WHAT THEY ARE

Just as there are twelve different signs in the complete zodiac, so there are twelve houses. But this is not a coincidence—the two are inter-linked. For example, Aries is the first sign in the zodiac and thus the first house exhibits many typically Aries concerns—physical body and its type, individual mannerisms, initial personality impact on the world at large. It is also the house which bears the Ascendant—sometimes called the rising sign—on its cusp. (More about this later.)

Each house further represents a specific area of every life, indicating in numerical succession the evolution of the self away from the purely personal concerns of the first house through to the intensely spiritual needs of the twelfth house. The houses themselves are numbered round the wheel (or circle) of the horoscope in a counter-clockwise direction as you'll observe in our illustration.

When you reach the stage of erecting a horoscope yourself, you'll note that each cusp (or spoke) of the horoscope wheel requires one of the twelve signs to be written against it. This will indicate precisely how the individual for whom the chart has been set up will handle the affairs of the house. Supposing your horoscope shows Capricorn on the cusp of the second—the house of income, financial matters and possessions. This implies a businesslike, organized approach to money which will be a constant problem to you if other factors in the horoscope promote spendthrift tendencies!

Our house diagram will give you the twelve house meanings at a glance but this is very basic—for quick reminder purposes only. You must understand each one in depth when your final aim is truly accurate interpretation. But, one last word on the houses themselves before we take our next step. They are each tagged as 'angular', 'succedent' or 'cadent'. So what does that add up to?

Angular or dominant houses

These are the first, fourth, seventh and tenth houses. Between them they represent the cornerstones of human existence: the self and its image (first); the home and its atmosphere (fourth); the marriage and the partner (seventh); and the career and its shape (tenth).

Check our house diagram (page 95) and you will note that the angular houses are marked by a small star. This is designed to remind students of the dominant role the angular houses play in chart interpretation, spotlighting how each individual will handle matters within the domain of each of these highly significant life areas.

To sum up: angular houses point to life areas—where the action is!

Succedent or following houses

These are the second, fifth, eighth and eleventh houses. Between them they postulate the immediate results which flow from circumstances set moving by the angular houses: personal finances and their state (second); creative efforts and their potential (fifth); moneys from others and their uses (eighth); and friendships and their outcome (eleventh).

Their role in individual charts is not quite as easy to analyse as their predecessors, the angular houses. But money and good contacts—as well as love—make the world go round, so succedent houses are far from being insignificant in overall effect.

To sum up: succedent houses point to life areas—where the profits are!

The twelve houses of the horoscope—at a glance

The dominant or angular houses 1-4-7-10 are marked by stars.

Quick-reference data

First house	= Individual personality projection.
Second house	= Personal income, financial affairs.
Third house	= Siblings, communication, mentality.
Fourth house	= Domestic scene, parental conditioning.
Fifth house	= Romantic liaisons, children, creativity.
Sixth house	= Working environment, health, service.
Seventh house	= Permanent unions, partnerships.
Eighth house	= Other people's assets, shared moneys, sexual conditioning.
Ninth house	= Long-distance travel, foreign-background persons, personal philosophies.
Tenth house	= Career, goal attainment, honours.
Eleventh house	= Friends, private hopes, group orientation.
Twelfth house	= Self-sacrifice, enmities, acts of self-undoing.
Angular houses	= Dominant houses, initiating action.
Succedent houses	= Following houses, reflecting results of action.
Cadent houses	= Dispersing houses, spreading of energies.

Cadent or dispersing houses

These are the third, sixth, ninth and twelfth houses. Between them they represent the final results which evolve from efforts applied through the succedent house areas: mental skills and their application (third); working aptitudes and their results (sixth); higher learning and its levels (ninth); self-abnegation and its rewards (twelfth).

The role of the cadent houses is patently far more subtle and far less immediately personal. But the demands of the ego, if relentlessly pursued at the expense of the paths which lead to spiritual evolution, offer little satisfaction in the end.

To sum up: cadent houses point to life areas—where the lessons are!

So, now we'll start our analysis of the twelve houses.

First house

This is an angular house and has a natural affinity with the sign of Aries and the planet Mars. It spotlights these life areas:
- Type of physical body, its strengths and weaknesses.
- Kind of environment into which each individual is born.
- First impressions made upon others.
- Extroverted or introverted behaviour.

Second house

This is a succedent house and has a natural affinity with the sign of Taurus and the planet Venus. It spotlights these life areas:
- Money, income-earning, material possessions.
- Adult financial status and utilization of money.
- Attitude towards financial obligations.
- What items or needs money is spent upon.

Third house

This is a cadent house and has a natural affinity with the sign of Gemini and the planet Mercury. It spotlights these life areas:
- Type and direction of intellectual/educational skills.
- Manner of communication of ideas.
- Relationship to brothers and sisters (if any) and their roles in

the life of the individual concerned.
- Aptitude for logical perceptive reasoning.

Fourth house
This is an angular house and has a natural affinity with the sign of Cancer and the Moon. It spotlights these life areas:
- Type of home and overall domestic scene throughout the entire life.
- Effect of parental conditioning in childhood years and its role in adult behaviour.
- Deeply ingrained habit patterns and emotional expression, resulting from early teaching.
- Situations surrounding the self during latter part of life.

Fifth house
This is a succedent house and has a natural affinity with the sign of Leo and the Sun. It spotlights these life areas:
- Inherent powers of creativity and their direction of expression.
- Approach to romantic opportunities and type of love affairs.
- Desire for pleasures and type most appreciated.
- Attitude towards children and chances of parenthood.

Sixth house
This is a cadent house and has a natural affinity with the sign of Virgo and the planet Mercury. It spotlights these life areas:
- Working environment and attitude to work.
- Overall health conditions and concern with physical self-improvement.
- Taste in dress and expression of self through chosen attire.
- Willingness to give service to others as employer or employee.

Seventh house
This is an angular house and has a natural affinity with the sign of Libra and the planet Venus. It spotlights these life areas:
- Marriage and all forms of permanent relationships.
- Type of mate which will be attracted.
- Capacity or incapacity to co-operate in close relationships.

● Potential for popular appeal and public support.

Eighth house

This is a succedent house and has a natural affinity with the sign of Scorpio and the planets Mars and Pluto. It spotlights these life areas:

● All moneys that involve other people's assets—inheritance, jointly held property, marital assets, corporate moneys.
● Aptitude for self-regeneration through mental and spiritual disciplines.
● Sexual conditioning carried over from childhood influences.
● Concern with death and the afterlife.

Ninth house

This is a cadent house and has a natural affinity with the sign of Sagittarius and the planet Jupiter. It spotlights these life areas:

● Opportunities or lack of them for overseas travel and long journeys.
● Interest in higher forms of education, publishing and sharing of knowledge.
● Type of philosophy acquired and religious interests.
● Involvement with others of foreign background and relatives by marriage.

Tenth house

This is an angular house and has a natural affinity with the sign of Capricorn and the planet Saturn. The tenth house spotlights these life areas:

● Type of profession/occupation sought and status therein.
● Personal reputation in career and likelihood of attaining fame or distinction therein.
● Capacity for concentrated effort and self-discipline in career attainments.
● Involvements with power figures in public or private affairs.

Eleventh house

This is a succedent house and has a natural affinity with the sign of Aquarius and the planet Uranus. The eleventh house spotlights these life areas:

- Type of friends and love attracted.
- Ability to work creatively in group activities and community affairs.
- Personal hopes and fulfilment of most important wishes.
- Type of social activities and interest therein.

Twelfth house

This is a cadent house and has a natural affinity with the sign of Pisces and the planet Neptune. The twelfth house spotlights these life areas:

- Subconscious repressions, emotional blocks and personal limitations.
- Willingness to sacrifice the self for the needs of others.
- Possibility of isolation and withdrawal from society.
- Hidden enmities from within the self or from others.

As we pointed out with the planetary meanings in Chapter 2, you do need, in the early stages of study, to learn the house meanings thoroughly. Later, when you've become accomplished in chart analysis, you'll acquire a feel for the houses too, and this naturally makes the synthesis (or blending) of chart traits much easier and much more fluent. This ability will come to you and every other student who applies the mind faithfully and notches up experience by erecting as many charts as humanly possible.

When I, myself, first began my studies in astrology many years ago, that is exactly what I did. Charts for anyone and everyone I knew—comparing the textbook theory to living people, and noting what personality traits were emphasized and how these affected the life-style, career, love relationships, etc. My own chart told me precisely (and a trifle bluntly I thought at the time) why I had screwed things up in the past. It introduced me in its own impartial way to parts of my own psychological make-up I didn't want to meet. But it is these, the unflattering, uneasy, uncooperative negative traits in ourselves we all have to tackle if we're going to change them into positive traits and apply our talents towards genuine fulfilment in life and love.

Anyway, we now hold in our hands quite a few of the numerous pieces that make up the complex jigsaw puzzle that is each human personality. Some of the pieces are big, some small; some bright, some dark; some smooth, some jagged. Some so closely identical they are almost repetitive; some so oddly dissimilar they look as if they're never going to fit anywhere in the puzzle. Among the pieces we can now recognize are the signs, the planets and their relationships to the signs.

We can recognize the influence of the houses too. So our next step is to place the planets into the houses of the horoscope. When you start to erect your own charts, you'll observe at once that often several houses are unoccupied by planets. These empty houses do not mean that the specific life area they spotlight is insignificant or that nothing will ever happen in it. They merely mean that that particular life area is not stressed in any way—neither helped nor hindered by planetary forces.

To illustrate: an empty fifth house does not infer that you will never have children, any more than an empty seventh house signifies that you will have no marriages or relationships. In such cases, the self does not have to concentrate its strongest energies on children or marriage: they do not represent a special problem.

THE PLANETS IN THE TWELVE HOUSES

Now, we're ready to fit the next set of pieces into the jigsaw of human personality—and they're very important pieces indeed.

Any planet occupying any house of the horoscope directs powerful energies into all the specific life areas indicated by that house. These energies can be constructive or destructive in their impact on each life, depending on how each individual handles them, and according to the aspects (or contacts) the planets make with each other. (Aspects will be discussed in detail in a later chapter.)

It virtually goes without saying that planets occupying the four angular houses in a chart will be more noticeably forceful in their impact because the most personal life areas are thus being forcefully stimulated. On the other hand, if none of the four angular houses in a chart contains planets—and this sometimes happens—the individual will experience less need to struggle endlessly for what he/she defines as happiness and achievement.

Of course, when all four angular houses are being constantly stressed by planets therein, the individual is forced into a lifelong juggling act: bouncing the demands for self-expression against the co-operation required in relationships; tossing the search for the right kind of home base, up against thrust for the right type of career. Never easy, never exactly comfortable—especially for those who had in mind a peaceful, jogtrot existence. But this planetary set-up as good as guarantees nobody's going to have time to get bored! They'll be much too busy trying to keep all four 'balls' in the air at once!

Direction of individual expression as shown by Sun house

Sun in 1st: ⊙ 1
A first house emphasis puts the spotlight on *self*, developing a brighter, sunnier form of self-expression. But will always need to watch egotistical behaviour and overstress on personal dignity.

Sun in 2nd: ⊙ 2
A second house emphasis puts the spotlight on *money and possessions* as important aids to self-expression. But will always need to watch money-mindedness and overstress on material gain.

Sun in 3rd: ⊙ 3
A third house emphasis puts the spotlight on *mentality* and contact with bright, intellectual types as important aids to self-expression. But will always need to watch superficial judgements and chopping and changing of ideas.

Sun in 4th: ⊙ 4
A fourth house emphasis puts the spotlight on *the home* as the main area of self-expression. But will always need to watch overstress on security and stick-in-the-mud attitudes, which can limit objectives.

Sun in 5th: ☉ 5

A fifth house emphasis puts the spotlight on *love affairs*, children and creative skills as a major area of self-expression. But will always need to watch tendencies to dominate and over-indulge own whims.

Sun in 6th: ☉ 6

A sixth house emphasis puts the spotlight on *work*, conscientiousness, and physical hygiene as important aids to self-expression. But will always need to watch tendency to overstress service to others and needless worry over physical condition.

Sun in 7th: ☉ 7

A seventh house emphasis puts the spotlight on *marriage* and partnership as the major area of self-expression. But will always need to watch tendency to expect too much from relationships and opportunistic conduct.

Sun in 8th: ☉ 8

An eighth house emphasis puts the spotlight on the search for *understanding* of life through psychic ability and mysticism. But will always need to watch tendency to overstress own sexual needs and sometimes obsessive interest in death and the afterlife.

Sun in 9th: ☉ 9

A ninth house emphasis puts the spotlight on *extensive travel*, idealism and sometimes religious concepts as major areas of self-expression. But will always need to watch tendency to exaggerate own mental abilities and achievements.

Sun in 10th: ☉ 10

A tenth house emphasis puts the spotlight on *success and career* as the major area of self-expression. But will always have to watch tendency to overstress personal prominence and status.

Sun in 11th: ☉ 11

An eleventh house emphasis puts the spotlight on the acquisition of *glamorous or influential friends* as important aids to self-expression. But will always need to watch over-reliance on own charm and tendency to 'collect' glamorous acquaintances.

Sun in 12th: ⊙ 12
A twelfth house emphasis puts the spotlight on *personal identity* through introspection and periods of seclusion. But will always need to watch tendency to hide from reality and confrontation with others.

Direction of emotional responses as shown by Moon house

Moon in 1st: ☽ 1
A first house emphasis directs your emotional energies into the attainment of a *strong desire for personal recognition*. This attitude makes you over-eager to please and apt to give too much for too little.

Moon in 2nd: ☽ 2
A second house emphasis directs your emotional energies towards the attainment of *money and possessions for the personal security* they bring. You tend to veer between being extremely careful and over-generous with family money.

Moon in 3rd: ☽ 3
A third house emphasis directs your emotional energies towards *a world of dreams and imagination*. Any type of routine relationship becomes boring very swiftly. You find it hard to maintain continuity or staying power.

Moon in 4th: ☽ 4
A fourth house emphasis directs your emotional energies primarily into the development of a *happy meaningful home life*. Family relationships are always a major consideration and disputes thus create deep and bitter hurts.

Moon in 5th: ☽ 5
A fifth house emphasis directs your emotional energies towards a constant *search for pleasures and romantic adventures*. Personal charm is boosted but moods are vacillating so it is hard to concentrate feelings on one person for long.

Moon in 6th: ☽ 6
A sixth house emphasis directs your emotional energies more

towards *harmony in the work environment* than in personal affairs. There is always a strong pressure towards the practical answer to emotional problems.

Moon in 7th: ☽ 7
A seventh house emphasis directs your emotional energies towards the search for a *mate who can fill a supportive or protective role*. You are extremely sensitive and responsive to the needs of others—especially if you are living with them in any form of permanent union.

Moon in 8th: ☽ 8
An eighth house emphasis directs your emotional energies into *unusual sensitivity to the needs of others and social currents* generally. It is vital to control your impressionability and learn to live a little more impersonally.

Moon in 9th: ☽ 9
A ninth house emphasis directs your emotional energies into attachment to *religious, social and ethical values instilled in early childhood*. You may needlessly limit your scope by identifying too closely with the attitudes and ideas of your own parents.

Moon in 10th: ☽ 10
A tenth house emphasis directs your emotional energies into *public relationships and personal achievement rather than domestic joys*. As a result, you gain the kind of acclaim you seek but often at the expense of deeper emotional fulfilment.

Moon in 11th: ☽ 11
An eleventh house emphasis directs your emotional energies into *the pursuit of friendships with women* who can also help you attain your objectives. You would usually have a very wide circle of acquaintances, but are not likely to accept intimate ties on a long-term basis.

Moon in 12th: ☽ 12
A twelfth house emphasis directs your emotional energies into *great sensitivity and moodiness*. The subconscious is very active and makes you react too impressionably to the opinions or behaviour of

intimates. Self-sacrifices are often called for.

Direction of mental activity as shown by Mercury house

Mercury in 1st: ☿ 1
A first house emphasis of Mercury directs your mental energies into fields where your *intellectual vitality, adaptable thinking* processes and alert reactions bring rewards. But your decisions can appear misdirected through jittery behaviour and nervous tension.

Mercury in 2nd: ☿ 2
A second house emphasis of Mercury directs your mental energies towards the *achievement of financial gain*, and ideas in this field are easily and quickly communicated. But decisions can appear overly cautious and materialistic.

Mercury in 3rd: ☿ 3
A third house emphasis of Mercury directs your mental energies towards *learning unusual skills* and boosts the powers of easy communication with others. Problems often exist with contemporary relatives, and ties to them are close, if not restricting.

Mercury in 4th: ☿ 4
A fourth house emphasis of Mercury directs your mental energies to *the home environment* and continuing (often unnecessary) anxiety about domestic affairs. But the mind requires to be concentrated on broader concepts than those of your immediate environment.

Mercury in 5th: ☿ 5
A fifth house emphasis of Mercury directs your mental energies rather too much towards *pleasure and love affairs in early maturity*. Later, the mental focus turns towards children, speculative investments, and artistic expression.

Mercury in 6th: ☿ 6
A sixth house emphasis of Mercury directs your mental energies towards *achievement through work* but with a restless desire for frequent change in mental activities. This creates a tendency to overstrain the physical resources and worry needlessly.

Mercury in 7th: ☿ 7
A seventh house emphasis of Mercury directs your mental energies towards *love partnerships*, which afford intellectual rather than emotional stimulation. The need is to try to develop greater emotional empathy, as a close relationship needs to be based on more than intellectual assessments.

Mercury in 8th: ☿ 8
An eighth house emphasis of Mercury directs your mental energies into *needless worrying over disagreements* and concern over the partner's financial resources after marriage. Inherited money through parents or parental relatives is a strong possibility.

Mercury in 9th: ☿ 9
A ninth house emphasis of Mercury directs your mental energies towards *the attainment of higher education* and tends to make you look always towards the future—sometimes at the expense of present circumstances. In-laws can amount to a communication problem.

Mercury in 10th: ☿ 10
A tenth house emphasis of Mercury directs your mental energies almost exclusively towards *the advancement of career* or whatever is the most desired material goal. Speedy results are more attractive to you than long-range plans. Decisions can be too hastily taken.

Mercury in 11th: ☿ 11
An eleventh house emphasis of Mercury directs your mental energies towards *the acquisition of helpful friends*, who are chosen mainly for their intelligence. Greater persistence in the use of mental powers is needed to realize your objectives fully.

Mercury in 12th: ☿ 12
A twelfth house emphasis of Mercury directs your mental energies into *subtle, secretive, private pursuits* in which you can investigate the mysteries of life. This often indicates that you are not properly understood by relatives or those in your personal environment.

Direction of affectional energies as shown by Venus house

Venus in 1st: ♀ 1
A first house emphasis directs your affectional energies into the *creation of harmonious, orderly surroundings*. Venus here also markedly increases personal charm and pleasantness of manner, but often indicates reliance on these traits.

Venus in 2nd: ♀ 2
A second house emphasis directs your affectional energies towards the provision of the *most beautiful, luxurious home money can buy*. Extravagance coupled with an insistent urge to improve social status can lead to errors of judgement in love.

Venus in 3rd: ♀ 3
A third house emphasis directs your affectional energies into the pursuit of *happy, harmonious domestic relationships* and an artistically attractive background. There is, however, often the wish to be pleasant and to please, but without too much effort.

Venus in 4th: ♀ 4
A fourth house emphasis directs your affectional energies towards domestic life and adds *further attachment to the home scene*. You tend to lean at times overly on spouse or immediate family instead of branching out yourself.

Venus in 5th: ♀ 5
A fifth house emphasis directs your affectional energies towards *short-lived exciting love affairs*. It intensifies your appeal to the opposite sex, but inclines you to expect romantic liaisons to run much too smoothly.

Venus in 6th: ♀ 6
A sixth house emphasis directs your affectional energies towards *those who share your work environment*, promoting popularity. This can divert your feelings away from personal involvement.

Venus in 7th: ♀ 7
A seventh house emphasis directs your affectional energies towards the *establishment of harmonious relationships* in all types of

partnership situations. This promises happiness in marriage provided the desire to protect, care for and co-operate with those you love is not overdone.

Venus in 8th: ♀ 8
An eighth house emphasis directs your affectional energies into situations which bring about *improvement in your financial status* through the efforts of those who love you. Overstress on sensuality and a lack of discipline in feelings need to be watched.

Venus in 9th: ♀ 9
A ninth house emphasis directs your affectional energies towards *harmonious relationships with intimates* and attraction to foreign-born partners. Pleasures of travel can be overstressed and exaggerated.

Venus in 10th: ♀ 10
A tenth house emphasis directs your affectional energies towards *acquiring success and prestige before the public*. A warm and friendly approach is shown to the world more easily than to intimates.

Venus in 11th: ♀ 11
An eleventh house emphasis directs your affectional energies into *happy relationships with friends* who can help you attain your objectives. You attract the affection of a wide variety of intelligent people but prefer ease to depth in relationships.

Venus in 12th: ♀ 12
A twelfth house emphasis directs your affectional energies towards *secret love involvements and clandestine affairs*. You are innately kind and sympathetic towards those loved but your own feelings are too often and much too easily hurt.

Direction of sexual energies as shown by Mars house

Mars in 1st: ♂ 1
A first house emphasis directs your physical energies into *intense forms of activity*. Self-assertion, physical strength and positivity are all boosted but problems arise through impulsiveness, over-

independence, haste and inability to play a submissive role in relationships.

Mars in 2nd: ♂ 2

A second house emphasis directs your physical energies towards *earning money* by concentrated effort and enterprising moves. This attitude arises from the feeling that financial status will make you a more attractive sexual partner but nevertheless directs energy away from personal involvement.

Mars in 3rd: ♂ 3

A third house emphasis directs your physical energies into *highly strung, nervous activity*. You are inclined to think more about sex than simply enjoy it. Satisfying sexual relationships cannot be thus 'intellectualized'. Less talk and more action is required.

Mars in 4th: ♂ 4

A fourth house emphasis directs your physical energies into an *urge for security* and a close involvement with home affairs. Sometimes there is a touch of the parental in the expression of feeling which is comforting and reassuring to many types of mates. However, you can be over-protective, thus creating discordant situations.

Mars in 5th: ♂ 5

A fifth house emphasis directs your physical energies towards *force and impulsiveness* in the expression of deeply felt desires. It intensifies the pursuit of pleasures and romantic involvements but often leads to conflict through the assumption of an argumentative stance towards partners.

Mars in 6th: ♂ 6

A sixth house emphasis directs your physical energies towards *satisfaction through personal achievement* at work and thus thrusts them away from personal situations. Both dynamic and active in 'getting things done', you very easily become impatient and irritable with less energetic partners and this attitude needs to be controlled.

Mars in 7th: ♂ 7

A seventh house emphasis directs your physical energies into *establishing a quick and early union* through marriage. However, because of the fiery and combative nature of Mars, the relationship is usually stormy and workable compromises require great self-restraint to achieve.

Mars in 8th: ♂ 8
An eighth house emphasis directs your physical energies into *the production of intense though often inhibited physical activities*. Disputes and difficulties can arise over any partner's money, stemming originally from misunderstandings in the field of sexual activity.

Mars in 9th: ♂ 9
A ninth house emphasis directs your physical energies towards *involvements with foreign born persons and excitement through travel*. Marked enthusiasm and impulse in sexual activities is shown. But also difficulties with partner's relatives often occur.

Mars in 10th: ♂ 10
A tenth house emphasis directs your physical energies more towards the *attainment of worldly success* than the achievement of private satisfaction. As both ambition, self-reliance and initiative are stimulated, it is very hard for you to blend in easily with a partner's demands.

Mars in 11th: ♂ 11
An eleventh house emphasis directs your physical energies into the *acquisition of a wide circle of valuable friends*, who can assist you in the achievement of your private goals, but there is often an associated lack of caution in the choice of close associates. Social life is often over-emphasized at the expense of private or physical satisfactions.

Mars in 12th: ♂ 12
A twelfth house emphasis directs your physical energies towards *involvement in secret sexual liaisons* usually caused by the fear of opposition from others. Along with this goes the urge to live in a world of romantic hopes and dreams rather than face up to realities, particularly the human imperfections of those who attract you.

Direction of opportunities to succeed
as shown by Jupiter house

Jupiter in 1st: ♃ 1

A first house emphasis directs the energies required to utilize opportunities towards *greater optimism and sociability so that advancement becomes easier*. Leadership abilities are well developed, as is self-confidence, but care must be taken to ensure they do not create egotism or insincerity. Over-optimism or over-generosity are twin problems.

Jupiter in 2nd: ♃ 2

A second house emphasis directs the energies required to utilize opportunities towards success through *speculation and the ability to sell your ideas to others*. Money and resources come to you relatively easily throughout life but you are not likely to be a saver. Extravagance is often a marked feature.

Jupiter in 3rd: ♃ 3

A third house emphasis directs the energies required to utilize opportunities towards *mental work of the type where you can use your powerful intuition and educational skills*. Often also implies an early environment that was conducive to mental development. Benefits come through pleasant relationships with contemporary relatives.

Jupiter in 4th: ♃ 4

A fourth house emphasis directs the energies required to utilize opportunities towards the *attainment of a happy, well-appointed and comfortable home background*. Both domestic happiness and abundance of money should have been established by middle age and remain for the rest of your life.

Jupiter in 5th: ♃ 5

A fifth house emphasis directs the energies required to utilize opportunities into creative activities and work relating to *investments, education or entertainments*. Still, care should be taken with all forms of financial speculation as you have a marked tendency to over-extend your physical and financial resources.

Jupiter in 6th: ♃ 6
A sixth house emphasis directs the energies required to utilize opportunities towards benefits from persons in *influential or authoritative* positions, involved with you through your working environment. Over-use of physical resources needs to be checked as approach to work can be over-enthusiastic.

Jupiter in 7th: ♃ 7
A seventh house emphasis directs the energies required to utilize opportunities into *social activities and co-operation* with others in teamwork or partnerships. Most kinds of sharing relationships with others work to your final advantage, including marital, but religious or cultural differences can create problems.

Jupiter in 8th: ♃ 8
An eighth house emphasis directs the energies required to utilize opportunities to *money received through partners or by way of inheritance*. It implies skill in handling family assets and other people's money, although there is an innate tendency towards extravagance. Emotional assessments and/or sexual drives can stir up trouble in business affairs if not kept in check.

Jupiter in 9th: ♃ 9
A ninth house emphasis directs the energies required to utilize opportunities into activities related to *long-distance travel, advanced intellectual pursuits* and sometimes publishing. Further expansion is likely through help from spouse's or business partner's relatives, provided tendency to expect too much from them is curbed.

Jupiter in 10th: ♃ 10
A tenth house emphasis directs the energies required to utilize opportunities towards achievements in *career fields* and adds natural expansiveness to the personal manner which attracts others to you. Also implies your moral standards at work are high and should ensure success—if you pursue it instead of trusting to luck too much.

Jupiter in 11th: ♃ 11
An eleventh house emphasis directs the energies required to utilize opportunities towards the achievements of *goals shared with friends*

or in group activities both of which are often numerous. Others are always willing to help you, so a high level of co-operation and mutual consideration ensues—provided you don't develop overly strong reliance on friends.

Jupiter in 12th: ♃ 12
A twelfth house emphasis directs the energies required to utilize opportunities towards success in *work connected with research* or related to hospitals and large institutions. Marked successes in all life sectors usually arrive in middle age but prior to then many opportunities are offered through friends or former enemies who have changed into friends. Problems can arise, however, from legal or religious matters.

Direction of success drives as shown by Saturn house

Saturn in 1st: ♄ 1
A first house emphasis directs your success drives towards *achievement through hard work* and an unrelenting determination to obtain recognition. Gives a very mature outlook on life even at a young age, together with a high level of self-discipline. There is a risk of self-centredness, however, usually stemming from a feeling of being unappreciated in childhood.

Saturn in 2nd: ♄ 2
A second house emphasis directs your success drives towards a *slow, painstaking building for the future*. You plan your resources carefully, often become needlessly anxious about finances and thus equally over-economize. Dangers to be watched are: too much materialism in your sense of values, together with difficulties in sharing.

Saturn in 3rd: ♄ 3
A third house emphasis directs your success drives towards *the pursuit of learning* and produces 'the perennial student' type. The sense of justice is keen and strong: exceptional patience is displayed in the achievement of important objectives. Also threatens over-conservatism, depressive moods and difficult communication with family members.

Saturn in 4th: ♄ 4

A fourth house emphasis directs your success drives towards *managerial situations* and thus implies you will have to accept heavy responsibilities in the achievement of your goals. Awkward early home experiences, older parents or anxiety about own old age can present problems which can curb gainful effort.

Saturn in 5th: ♄ 5

A fifth house emphasis directs your success drives towards *obtaining authority over others* and prominence in the creative field. However, this does exercise an inhibiting influence on the flow of creative imagination and self-expression which can only be overcome by thinking more of others and less of the circumscribed area of your own desires.

Saturn in 6th: ♄ 6

A sixth house emphasis directs your success drives towards *success through some form of demanding employment*. It stimulates the capacity for hard work, often to the point where you can become too hard on yourself and others. This does not make it really easy for you to blend into a work environment because you tend to stand apart from workmates.

Saturn in 7th: ♄ 7

A seventh house emphasis directs your success drives into *situations where difficulties in relationships and partnerships force you to learn the lessons of co-operation or face disappointment*. An intense desire for security produces 'lone wolf' attitudes and sometimes a delayed or awkward marriage. A deep emotional sensitivity or 'touchiness' is kept hidden under a self-controlled front.

Saturn in 8th: ♄ 8

An eighth house emphasis directs your success drives towards *a continuing search for deeper understanding* of yourself and your own motivations. It implies difficulties in financial affairs with all types of partners and limits possibility of gain through assets of others or inheritance. Also suggests a concealed sensuality which requires control.

Saturn in 9th: ♄ 9

A ninth house emphasis directs your success drives towards *involvement with overseas countries, foreign-born persons and foreign cultures*. In the early life it also produces very rigid attitudes towards objectives but a more flexible philosophy emerges in the later years. Problems to watch are: too exacting demands on others and intolerance.

Saturn in 10th: ♄ 10

A tenth house emphasis directs your success drives towards *work which will improve your position* in the social scale, coupled with a powerful desire for money and personal prestige. Early successes, self-reliance and good business ability are indicated but too much pride is always a clear danger which must be watched.

Saturn in 11th: ♄ 11

An eleventh house emphasis directs your success drives towards *goals and objectives which appear unattainable* but in fact *can* be achieved through patience and unremitting effort. Financial rewards are invariably much better in later life. Many acquaintances but few friends are likely due to a concealed fear of the demands of friendship.

Saturn in 12th: ♄ 12

A twelfth house emphasis directs your success drives into *a deep-seated, but sometimes unrecognized, need to serve others*, and sets up the necessity for periods of solitude in which goals and objectives can be formulated and reconsidered. Often develops a subconscious fear, which shows itself in the tendency to imagine position or aims are being threatened by others.

Direction of individualism as shown by Uranus house

Uranus in 1st: ♅ 1

A first house emphasis postulates an exceptionally strong *individuality*—very original in ideas and methods of working. Personal code of ethics is strong, firm but unconventional. Thus often misunderstood by others and may feel a recurring sense of isolation and restlessness. Needs to overcome the wilfulness inherent in this position.

Uranus in 2nd: ♅ 2

A second house emphasis postulates *financial circumstances* affected suddenly and unexpectedly by unforeseen circumstances throughout life. Result is many ups and downs in income or financial affairs generally. Probably gets highly original ideas about making money—inventive flashes as to business advancement.

Uranus in 3rd: ♅ 3

A third house emphasis postulates *environmental difficulties* in early years and later wilful or rebellious reactions. Severe upsets in the home during adolescence likely. Very mentally restless type. Conflicts with fraternal relatives possible. Probably lacks genuine concentration though mind is quick and agile.

Uranus in 4th: ♅ 4

A fourth house emphasis postulates *unsettled or difficult conditions in childhood*. Many changes of home possible. Not really a domestic type and does not want a fixed, established home environment. Sudden, unexpected changes break up any crystallized patterns of existence from time to time.

Uranus in 5th: ♅ 5

A fifth house emphasis postulates *tendencies towards reckless, foolhardy behaviour* in respect of romantic relationships. Usually, over-strong assertion of individualism and independence. Children likely to be original, independent and unusual. Need for restraint on self-assertion.

Uranus in 6th: ♅ 6

A sixth house emphasis postulates *capability* for high standard work but detests routine. Very ingenious and original in solving work problems. Cannot take prolonged work in dull jobs or becomes nervous and irritable. Tends to have extremist attitude to all work forms. Either over-exerts the self mercilessly or baulks at what has to be done.

Uranus in 7th: ♅ 7

A seventh house emphasis postulates *difficult but unusual and exciting conditions in marriage*, partially caused by very strongly developed sense of independence. Likely to attract spouse who is unconventional and also resents the restrictions and responsibilities of marriage. Would find it equally difficult to work with others in partnership situations. Divorce or separations often occur with Uranus here.

Uranus in 8th: ♅ 8
An eighth house emphasis indicates that *sudden and surprising events* throughout life are likely where partnerships, legacies or other forms of inherited assets are concerned. Needs to exercise great care and forethought before entering into any type of partnership. Intuitions strong and psychic experience possible.

Uranus in 9th: ♅ 9
A ninth house emphasis postulates *chance of success* in any matters relating to *foreign countries or foreign-born persons*. Rather unorthodox attitude to religion and unusual religious views. Possible difficulties with in-laws. Likely to marry spouse who was not born in own country. Could make long trips, possibly overseas, at some time.

Uranus in 10th: ♅ 10
A tenth house emphasis postulates deep-seated *unconventionality*. Not a conformer. Highly individualistic. Dislikes taking orders from anyone. Insists on career where can be own boss. Altruistic, humanitarian reactions in general outlook. Responds best to indirect approach. Some very peculiar, unorthodox concepts about own objectives.

Uranus in 11th: ♅ 11
An eleventh house emphasis postulates *open-mindedness* and the desire for truth at all costs. Tradition or approval are of little concern in psychological make-up, so likely to take an unorthodox, even bohemian, approach to any type of physical relationship. Friends are usually two distinct types: the very conventional and the very 'way-out'.

Uranus in 12th: ♅ 12
A twelfth house emphasis postulates a tremendous, deep-seated urge to feel *free of restrictions*. But at the same time develops a sense of being constantly confined by events or actions of others. Often

'loner' types who unless they exercise great self-control, can become their own worst enemies, and thus lose out on many opportunities.

Direction of intuitive understanding as shown by Neptune house

Neptune in 1st: ♆ 1

A first house emphasis adds an *extremely sensitive awareness* of the self and personal environment. It makes for a very high degree of impressionability towards the ideas and attitudes of others, which can sometimes work to disadvantage. The indicated need is to develop the higher mind.

Neptune in 2nd: ♆ 2

A second house emphasis adds *difficulties with finances* throughout life. Alternating gains and losses for no clearly apparent reason. Easily deceived by others in any matters relating to money. Should be on guard for various types of trickery with finances.

Neptune in 3rd: ♆ 3

A third house emphasis adds an *artistic, imaginative dimension* in the overall mentality which may be unrealized or suppressed. Can show itself through lack of concentration during school years which reduces educational prowess. Probable troubles with fraternal relatives.

Neptune in 4th: ♆ 4

A fourth house emphasis adds likelihood of *vaguely unsettled home conditions* and the need for a more than usual amount of self-sacrifice on the domestic scene. Also often suggests mysteries and secrets in respect of the family origin and marked idealism about the childhood home and the parents.

Neptune in 5th: ♆ 5

A fifth house emphasis adds *lack of freedom in expression of emotions*. Romantic affairs likely to be secret or, in some subtle way, restricted by circumstances. Likely to make great sacrifices for own children but may feel unappreciated. Vivid imagination which may often overcome common sense.

Neptune in 6th: ♆ 6
A sixth house emphasis adds *super-sensitivity* and a high degree
of suggestibility—especially in regard to negative feelings emanating
from other persons in the environment. It is vital to look for a happy
working situation with compatible people as conflict or disharmony
in the occupational area can be very destructive.

Neptune in 7th: ♆ 7
A seventh house emphasis adds an *unrealistic attitude to marriage*
and love partnerships—the 'rosy spectacles' picture. Should try
to be less idealistic in hopes for marital bliss but will always be
attracted to out-of-the-ordinary types.

Neptune in 8th: ♆ 8
An eighth house emphasis adds *recurring financial difficulties in
business or marital relationships* through deception or trickery.
Possibility of legacies or gifts of family money later in life, but these
too are likely to be plagued by uncertainty. Likely to have very
vivid, sometimes precognitive dreams. Strange relationship with
parents or older family members possible.

Neptune in 9th: ♆ 9
A ninth house emphasis adds *quick and accurate intuitions* which
aid in sustained study or written work. There is usually a marked
interest in mysticism which does not always reveal itself till later
in life. Problems often occur with in-laws after marriage due to lack
of empathy. Peculiar situations arise related to foreigners or overseas
travel.

Neptune in 10th: ♆ 10
A tenth house emphasis adds *ambivalent attitudes to occupation*.
Often feels uncertain as to what own objectives in life really are.
Possible lack of guidance from father or difficulties in relationship
with him. In work situations often believes far more has been given
than received.

Neptune in 11th: ♆ 11
An eleventh house emphasis adds *difficulties and disappointments
through friends* who are often odd or unusual types. Vital to use
discrimination in choice of all close associates. Very easily deceived

or misled. Also indicates lack of clarity in life objectives. Apt to be a dreamer rather than an achiever if determination is not exercised.

Neptune in 12th: ♆ 12
A twelfth house emphasis adds a *deep-seated sense of loneliness* caused by extreme sensitivity at the subconscious level. Life circumstances are such that there is often a sensation of being confined in conditions from which it is hard to escape.

Direction of subconscious drives as shown by Pluto house

Pluto in 1st: ♇ 1
A first house emphasis postulates *struggle* against problems in childhood—emotional or physical. Feels the need to strive for survival throughout life. Can become very self-willed. Considerable initiative but finds it hard to co-operate with others or to conform. Very individualistic. Early life experiences have literally forced a transformation on total personality.

Pluto in 2nd: ♇ 2
A second house emphasis postulates remarkable *tenacity* in striving for material possessions and financial status—sometimes to the point of over-acquisitiveness. Financial gains can come suddenly or unusually. Probable adventurousness in handling money. Often very successful in speculation, discoveries, or inventions.

Pluto in 3rd: ♇ 3
A third house emphasis postulates an able, *penetrating mind* and an unwillingness to compromise on deeply held beliefs or convictions. Mental resourcefulness, scientific ability and originality of ideas are also implied. Difficulties with contemporary relatives occur from time to time throughout life.

Pluto in 4th: ♇ 4
A fourth house emphasis postulates strange or unusual *circumstances in the home* during childhood plus loss of, or difficulties with one parent. Also indicates intense desire to rule the home and the domestic scene. This needs to be watched or power struggles between family members may develop.

Pluto in 5th: ♇ 5
A fifth house emphasis postulates strong, *creative subconscious urges* expressed through artistic interests, hidden love involvements and the advancement of children. Because of intensity of interest in children there is danger of dominating them—of pushing square pegs into round holes.

Pluto in 6th: ♇ 6
A sixth house emphasis postulates subconscious urges to engage in *odd or strange occupations*. Deep, perhaps unrealized interest in the sciences and healing techniques. Capacity to achieve much in the chosen avenue of endeavour by the simplest means. Often interested in aiding sick or disadvantaged. Capable of conscientious, regenerative work.

Pluto in 7th: ♇ 7
A seventh house emphasis postulates a *married life* that is full of struggles, overturns, adventures and crises, designed to develop the character and the capacity to co-operate on the deepest subconscious levels with the partner. Also gives unusual creative abilities, strength and vitality.

Pluto in 8th: ♇ 8
An eighth house emphasis postulates a *powerful will*, sometimes combined with clairvoyant ability. Attitude to life as a whole is extremely serious. Little patience with trivialities or trivial people. Good personal strength and resourcefulness in times of crisis. Carries on many activities in secret. Possible problems with partner's money or obtaining inheritances.

Pluto in 9th: ♇ 9
A ninth house emphasis postulates a lifelong *desire to acquire knowledge*, learning and varied experiences. Also suggests the possibility of living a major part of the life in a country far from the place of birth. Adventurous, sensation-seeking attitudes insistently impel the self to explore new worlds.

Pluto in 10th: ♇ 10
A tenth house emphasis postulates a tenacious striving for *power and independence*, coupled with unusual enterprise in furthering

career goals and/or personal objectives. Also makes for a certain aggressiveness in attaining aims, which may create business enmities and fills the destiny pattern with unforeseen turning points and crises.

Pluto in 11th: P. 11

An eleventh house emphasis postulates subconscious urges towards *group activities* and numerous friendships with like-minded and very progressive people. The friends attracted after maturity are likely to be those in influential positions who can materially help in promoting whatever major objective is important at any given time.

Pluto in 12th: P. 12

A twelfth house emphasis postulates *periods of intense frustration*, arising out of the feeling that others misunderstand or misinterpret words or actions. At the same time, it gives a tendency to suppress or conceal the deeper emotions so that they suddenly burst out and can lead into unwise emotional or love links.

Quick-reference data
The Planets' Houses at a Glance

House	Area of influence
Sun	Individual expression
Moon	Emotional responses
Mercury	Mental activity
Venus	Affectional energies
Mars	Physical energies
Jupiter	Success opportunities
Saturn	Ambition drives
Uranus	Individualism
Neptune	Intuitive understanding
Pluto	Subconscious drives

By now, you're probably wondering how on earth you're ever going to be able to stack up—say, such a contradictory double as Saturn and Uranus rattling round together in the first house. Tough, restrictive, disciplinarian, conservative Saturn, and way-out, eccentric, non-conformist, forward-looking Uranus. Again, it's not as hopelessly confusing as it looks. In actual practice it's rather like mixing the varied ingredients of a cake. The nuts, the eggs, the flour, the sugar are all totally different commodities but they do blend into a cohesive whole. All you need is the right recipe and the right amount of know-how. In astrology, this final blending is termed 'synthesis'. There's no dodging the fact that successful synthesis of personality traits is the hardest part of your learning programme.

Accurate, expert summation of individual life patterns only comes with time and experience—never from a superficial glance at a chart or a rambling recital of textbook data. If you take either approach you'll discover—to extend our analogy further—you've turned what should have been a plumcake into a meringue!

Indeed, I recall two chart analyses shown me by clients a few years ago. Both were typewritten. Both their authors claimed to be professional astrologers. Both were expensive. The first 'analysis' was nothing more than a regurgitated torrent of old, out-of-date textbook definitions. Nothing synthesized. Everything glaringly contradictory (a sure sign of incompetence and/or laziness). The client was totally bamboozled by the tangled mess of personality traits and potentials and had been trying to make sense of it for years. The second 'analysis' was a weird and wonderful melange of fanciful statements such as 'Your soul inhabits a secret garden.' (Vagueness like that is a sure sign of a practitioner who is too fearful or too inexperienced to be definitive.)

All of this prompts another word of warning. If you plan to engage an astrologer yourself, always ask what his/her qualifications and experience are. Remember there are as yet no legal barriers preventing fakes or charlatans advertising in the press and calling themselves astrologers or astrological consultants. Some of them may have no more than the sketchiest knowledge of the science. (Another chart I saw which had been prepared by a self-styled 'professional' showed the client's birthtime as 6.50 a.m. but the Sun's position was for a birthtime around 9 p.m. That 'professional' didn't even know how to calculate!) These phonies do untold damage to the great science of astrology, leaving it open to scorn and dismissal by laymen.

But now, we've arrived at the stage where we can begin to pick up the final pieces of the jigsaw—the planetary aspects.

TEXT EXERCISES

1. Compare the life-style and interests of an individual whose chart shows:
   (a) planets occupying all four angular houses
   (b) only the first house stressed by planets
   (c) all the angular houses empty

2. In handling money matters, what differing types of demands and financial involvements would you expect from a marked planetary stress on the second house as opposed to the eighth?

3. Some individuals take to travel like ducks to water. Others avoid it if humanly possible. What planets in which houses and signs in your opinion produce the natural globe-trotter, and which the stay-at-home?

4. You are analysing a chart with Saturn occupying the first house. What sort of behaviour would you anticipate from the owner of this chart? And how would you counsel him/her in dealing with this kind of Saturnian influence?

5. The Sun in the seventh house is traditionally regarded as a beneficial influence in all the affairs of that house.
   (a) Describe the various meanings of the seventh house.
   (b) Discuss the behavioural responses of an individual to seventh house affairs when his/her chart shows the Sun in Leo in the seventh house.
   (c) What would you consider the effect of an empty seventh house to be in the life-purpose of a given individual?

6. In your own words, explain the differences in impact of the angular, succedent and cadent houses. Why do you think the angular houses are regarded as of greatest impact?

7. Assume you have been requested by a parent to advise on possible careers for a school-leaver. What added clues to talent and mental potential would you gather from:
   (a) Gemini on the tenth house cusp with both Uranus and Neptune in that house?

(b) Virgo on the tenth house cusp with the Sun, Venus and Mars in that house?

(c) Cancer on the tenth house cusp with Mercury and Pluto in that house?

8. Accurate astrological analysis relies on skilful synthesis of the many factors in each individual chart. In what order of significance would you place houses, planets and signs in attempting a synthesis? Give your reasons why.

9. In advising a couple on compatibility prior to marrying, to which houses in their charts would you give special emphasis? How would you assess their attitudes to children, acceptance of marital responsibilities, and capacity for fidelity in marriage —taking into consideration signs, houses and planets which influence these issues?

10. What planets in which houses would you associate with the following quotes?

(a) 'I can't remember anything much about my childhood. I don't like to think about it.'

(b) 'I expect freedom in marriage or relationships. I can't stand anyone crowding me. If they do, I leave.'

(c) 'Children? I adore children. I can't wait to have a family.'

(d) 'If I was a failure in my career, life wouldn't be worth living.'

(e) 'I'm an engineer but every so often I start wondering if I made a mistake. Maybe, I should have been an artist or a writer.'

(f) 'People are always crying on my shoulder. Sometimes it drives me mad but I can't stop myself from trying to help them—even when I know they don't deserve it.'

(g) 'From the time I was a little kid, I knew I wanted to be a soldier. I joined the regular army as soon as I was old enough and never looked back.'

MODEL ANSWERS

Note

The model answers given in the following pages are offered in fairly brief outline as guidance to each test participant. Your own answers do not have to be exactly the same to be marked as correct. Original thinking is always rewarded, provided that your ideas show you have learned and understood the basic tenets of astrological theory.

Q1

(a) A lifelong juggling act. Tremendous stimulation towards forceful action in all four major life sectors. No let-up, really, as the self strives to equate urge for self-expressive freedom against strong home commitment, the demands for co-operation in relationships against the search for career fulfilment. Tension often builds in times when the competing drives run into each other.

(b) The personality's own needs dominate the scene. Hence any attempt by others to baulk action in this life sector is likely to meet with forceful resistance. May give impression of self-centredness, the manner in which this will show depending on which planets are located in the first house.

(c) Nothing like the trials and learning indicated by (b) and (c). The self is allowed to apply its energies without constant goading from within or by external events. Basically, a much easier passage through life than (a) or (b), but possibly less outstanding achievement because such a need is not intensely felt.

Q2

Both houses, when stressed by planets, provoke marked concern with financial dealings.

The second, being the natural house of Taurus, picks up Taurean attitudes towards money—desire for it and possessiveness towards it. Material resources are used to provide a frame for the self-image. Little desire to share in financial deals organized by others.

The eighth, being the natural house of Scorpio, attracts money and possessions from others, often in the form of inheritance. The self is led inexorably into handling jointly held assets, advising on financial affairs to help others apply their resources, partnerships and the like. 'Going it alone' in financial affairs is a situation not easily arranged.

Q3

Basically, the third house rules short journeys and the ninth house long-distance travel. The planet Jupiter and the sign of Sagittarius produce the natural traveller type. Pluto in the ninth will provoke subconscious change brought about by exposure to foreign cultures. Gemini is also a sign which stimulates travel interest but more for purely intellectual titillation.

On the opposite side, earth signs rarely pursue travel with alacrity because the break in routine is instinctively disliked.

Saturn occupying the third and ninth houses inhibits travel possibilities and the inclination to use such opportunities when they do arise.

Q4

'Old head on young shoulders' type in childhood and early maturity. Doubts as to self-worth likely to show in prickliness, lack of confidence and a somewhat fearful approach to people and life itself. Parental influences likely to be unsatisfactory, leaving a residual sense of being both unloved and unlovable. Hence possible selfishness and self-absorption.

In counselling, greater optimism should be instilled—more willingness to trust others and to let the whole personality show, instead of keeping it under cover for fear of rejection. This type has a strong sense of responsibility, but dreary reactions and negativity have to be worked upon.

Q5

(a) Marital affairs, all permanent unions, including long-term business partnerships, public appeal. This house will often give indications of type of partner attracted, through its cusp and planets positioned therein. Also gives clues to each individual's reaction to permanent relationships.

(b) Any planet in seventh will infer lessons to be learnt through permanent unions with others. The Sun is always an irradiating influence, stressing the need to relate warmly. The sign of Leo often brings in dignified, powerful types as partners, but may also suggest an overly commanding/demanding attitude to relationships.

(c) Empty houses, of course, do not mean that these life sectors are insignificant. An empty seventh, however, does imply that the individual does not need marriage/union in order to develop potential. The strong pull towards permanent relationships is not present, although this does not suggest the individual will remain unattached for life.

Q6

Angular houses are the cornerstones of human existence. Tremendous force is added to whatever life sector is stressed by planets in these houses.

Succedent houses, as the name implies, are like followers, reflecting the results from their leaders—the angulars.

Cadent houses, to take another analogy, are rather like minor keys in music, pointing up the benefits of learning, acquiring a workable philosophy, putting the needs of others before the self's.

The angulars always dominate a chart when stressed because for most individuals the demands of self-projection, home, marriage and career largely determine the overall life-style. The ego force manifests most visibly in the angular houses.

Q7

(a) Versatility, communicative powers, people-orientation and dislike of desks and routine are common with Gemini in the tenth. Often a strong interest in some form of writing. Uranus there will hurl in an even greater multiplicity of career interests and possibly change career or its direction several times.

   Neptune, always deceptive, can offer marked artistic talent but cause the individual to doubt whether the career finally chosen was the right one. This doubt often continues throughout life.

   In my view, the counsellor should never be too definitive in career advice, indicating talents/potentials rather than specifying particular jobs.

(b) Analytical mind, interest in psychology, careers with practical foundations and leading to clear-cut job opportunities are all implied by Virgo in the tenth. Attraction to teaching or lecturing is also possible.

Strong planetary stress (small stellium) suggest career thrust is very powerful. The Sun here pushes towards power/prestige, hence suggesting authoritative behaviour. Venus here tones down this somewhat dictatorial approach by adding charm and smoothness with colleagues, co-workers, etc. Mars here reinforces the Sun with an almost militaristic drive for success.

(c) All the sensitive, moody, nurturing attitudes of Cancer focus themselves on the occupational field.

Often attracts to occupations linking with the medical or paramedical fields. Mercury in the tenth directs the mind towards intellectual, communicative work plus the pursuit of hard facts. Often implies too much speed in both expectation of success and efforts applied thereto. Pluto in the tenth can be somewhat problematical. This position projects an enormous demand for public recognition, rooted in subconscious drives, but frequently a dictatorial attitude that can alienate colleagues. There is an inclination to insist that only the self is right in occupational matters.

Q8

The *signs* themselves need to be considered first: they are visualized 'signposts', graphically pointing up the range of behavioural responses inherent in each individual.

The *planets* focus energy on particular signs, helping or hindering manifestation of traits according to the nature of the planet and whether or not that planet is comfortable in the sign it occupies in a birth chart.

The *houses* symbolizing the twelve departments of life show the channels through which planetary energy will be discharged.

All three areas have to be worked together into a detailed picture of personality when the synthesis is completed.

Q9

Firstly the angular houses in comparing the two charts. This shows whether the pair will wish to express in similar or conflicting life sectors. For example, a female with a stressed tenth house won't find it easy to reconcile her needs with those of a male who has a stressed fourth house.

For children—attitudes for or against—the fifth house, considering its cusp and planets occupying it. Special attention should be paid to planets in both charts stressing or making aspects to the fifth house. The fifth house again, coupled with the seventh house, give clues to the two individuals' expectation or otherwise of fidelity. The signs of the Moon, Venus and Mars plus aspects to them are further important indicators of how each partner views love, romance and marriage.

Acceptance of marital responsibilities often reflects childhood conditioning and early home influences—the fourth house. Tough planets therein and aspects to them are important. Equally a stressed first or tenth house can show the type whose strongest energies thrust towards the advancement of the self. If this need conflicts with marital responsibilities, the latter will suffer.

Q10

(a) Saturn in the fourth or first. Implies early life was not happy and repression of memory ensues.

(b) Uranus in the seventh and sometimes in the fifth. This planet tends to smash relationships abruptly if the partner becomes possessive or restricting. Pluto in the seventh also pulls against total co-operation with a partner.

(c) The Moon in the fifth very often. Venus in the fifth promotes pleasure through children but not quite the same emotional need for them as the Moon.

(d) Saturn in the tenth expressing the urge for achievement plus the determination to apply the self relentlessly towards career goals.

(e) Neptune in the tenth suggesting uncertainty as to career choice plus latent artistic/creative talents.

(f) Neptune in the twelfth, symbolizing the need to help those who cannot cope plus the inability to discriminate between those who will try to help themselves and those who won't.

(g) Mars in the tenth, showing the militancy of the planet expressing itself easily and literally.

4.

THE PLANETARY ASPECTS

RECOGNITION OF ASPECTS

In earlier times, when the average God-fearing citizen spent his days dogged by visions of eternal damnation, fiery pits and demons lurking round every corner, astrologers gave it to him hot and strong too.

Planets and their aspects were lumped into two big bundles: the 'benefics' with their reassuring 'good' aspects, and the 'malefics' with their blood-curdling, 'evil' aspects.

This hard-line and too simplistic division continued up into the early decades of the twentieth century when the modern doctrines of psychology began to infiltrate serious astrological writing, particularly through the researches of Professor Carl Jung (famed as the father of many modern psychoanalytic methods).

Jung's work and that of those who followed in his footsteps proved repeatedly that human free will plays a major role in handling planetary energies. That astrology is not and never was intended to be a fatalistic system of sooth-saying is a view—you'll be interested to hear—shared by Nostradamus, who wrote as far back as the sixteenth century.

Nostradamus, too, maintained that within the pattern of personality traits and events shown by the horoscope chart, there was always an area of choice—of handling a given situation in a negative, destructive manner, or getting on top of it through positive, constructive action.

Hence the once-called 'benefics' and 'good' aspects between planets do not rain down pennies from heaven upon your delighted head—unless you're quick enough to turn your umbrella upside down and catch them. Nor do the once-called 'malefics' and 'evil' aspects between planets hurl you willy-nilly over cliffs—if you refuse to be pushed to the edge.

Thus in counselling I much prefer to label 'favourable' and 'unfavourable' planetary aspects as 'easy' or 'challenging'. If you glance at our quick-reference table (page 135) you'll see their names, symbols and the degrees between them. These are the seven most widely used in astrological analysis. There are several lesser aspects but in my view they add little to the personality picture and often hopelessly confuse the novice. Indeed, the compiling of a mountainous heap of aspects is a common fault among beginners, who thereupon promptly lose themselves in the maze of possibilities it presents.

Getting your analysis right is a bit like drawing a relief map of a country. The mountain ranges, the deep valleys, the great rivers give us the clues as to the type of place it is—not the molehills, water-holes or little hollows. The same goes for each picture of human personality.

What an aspect is

In her lengthy and authoritative work entitled *The Modern Textbook of Astrology*, written in 1951 but still going strong, English astrologer Margaret Hone, Principal of the Faculty of Astrological Studies in London from 1945 to 1969, gives the excellent definition of aspects set out below:

> Astronomically, aspects are certain distances made at the centre of the Earth between a line from one planet and a line from another. These are measured in degrees along the ecliptic. Astrologically, their interpretative significance is all-important, as it qualifies the way in which the principles of the planets manifest.

Incidentally, her big, 320-page book is the one I often recommend to anyone starting their own astrological library. It is comprehensive, always clear, always accurate. If you have heard would-be fashionable practitioners or teachers dismissing such a work merely because it was first published more than thirty years ago, think again! All serious students and practitioners need to read regularly on new research and new advances in the field, but that does not mean authoritative, well-documented earlier books should be ignored.

Many conjunctions, and all trines and sextiles are tagged as 'easy' aspects: this means the planets' energies combine with each other comfortably. All oppositions, all squares and to a lesser extent the quincunxes are tagged as 'challenging' aspects: this means the planets' energies hammer away at each other relentlessly.

The semi-sextile—a minor aspect—is invariably mild in its effect, implying a vaguely disharmonious link between the planets involved, but not much else. Hence in general analysis it is rarely worth worrying about.

If you're a newcomer to astrological studies, the quincunx (also called inconjunct in some texts) is best left alone. It implies an incompatible link between the planets involved, creative of divergent attitudes that waste effort and set up 'cross-purposes' situations. Thus it is hard to assess for the inexperienced.

Whether a conjunction will be regarded as 'easy' or 'challenging' depends on the nature of the planets making the aspect. To illustrate: the Sun conjunct Saturn in a chart can put its owner through some pretty heavy learning as hard, restrictive Saturn tends to block the brightness of the Sun. On the other hand, the Sun conjunct Jupiter in a chart can give opportunities that pop up like mushrooms, as benevolent, expansive Jupiter boosts the brightness of the Sun.

Thus if you concentrate on the nature of any two planets making a conjunction, as set out in Chapter 2 you'll be able to decide whether such conjunction is easy or challenging.

In the definitions of planetary aspects which follow, I've kept them as concise as possible and placed them in their natural order, starting with the Sun and finishing with Mars. These five, you'll remember from earlier sections, are the planets exercising the most markedly personal influence on everyone's life. Aspects between the latter five—Jupiter through to Pluto—do not produce such visible effects in individual behaviour and hence are of lesser significance in overall personality assessment. Indeed, aspects between the outer planets Uranus, Neptune and Pluto are often termed 'generation aspects' because they appear in charts of large groups of humanity born at any given time, indicating underlying attitudes of the entire group.

Orbs of aspect

Some of the terminology of astrology often sounds odd and off-putting to beginners but not when you grasp the meanings. The term 'orb' is merely the word defining the space within which any given aspect will become operative. Certainly, from time to time marked controversies have raged among astrological authors as to the allowable degree of orb, but the following are those most widely accepted:

For *major aspects*—conjunctions, trines, squares and oppositions—the 8 degree orb applies.
For *minor aspects*—sextiles—the 6 degree orb applies; semi-sextiles—the 2 degree orb applies; quincunxes—the 2 degree orb applies.

Now, let's look at the orbs of the Sun in action with a few examples. Assume you have calculated a chart and find the personal planets in the degrees and minutes set out hereunder.

Sun = 10 degrees 15 minutes of Virgo
Moon = 5 degrees 56 minutes of Gemini
Mercury = 14 degrees 03 minutes of Libra
Venus = 24 degrees 14 minutes of Cancer
Mars = 16 degrees 28 minutes of Pisces

Applying the allowable orbs, the aspects are:

Sun = square Moon—orb within 8 degrees
Sun = no aspect to Mercury — beyond 2 degrees orb for semi-sextiles
Sun = no aspect to Venus—beyond 6 degree orb for sextiles
Sun = opposition Mars—orb being within 8 degrees

Of course, in the finished chart these Sun aspects would be written using the appropriate symbols, i.e.:

$$\odot \; 10:15 \; \text{♏}:$$
$$\odot \; \square \; \text{☽} : \; \text{♌} \; \text{♌}$$

Table of major aspects

Aspect	Degrees apart	Symbol	Interpretation
Conjunction	0-8	♂	Forceful
Semi-sextile	30	⊻	Slightly stressful
Sextile	60	✳	Easy
Square	90	□	Very stressful
Trine	120	Δ	Very easy
Quincunx	150	⊼	Divergent
Opposition	180	☍	Very tense

Hidden aspects

This type of aspect is one that beginners often miss because each aspect is judged by its orb. Hence, for example, two planets in water signs can form a square to each other instead of a trine in this manner.

Say, you have Mercury in a chart in 29 degrees of Cancer and Uranus in 2 degrees of Scorpio. Uranus is thus just out of Libra and the orb between the degree of Mercury and the degree of Uranus is only 3 degrees. The sign of Cancer squares the sign of Libra, so the above-mentioned aspect is a square.

If you're not all that mathematically minded, you'll find aspect assessment much easier if you recheck the relationships between the signs of the zodiac we discussed in Chapter 1.

So here follows a quick reference reminder list. But never forget an aspect only counts if the planets involved are *within orb*—i.e., within 8 degrees of each other for major aspects or within 2 to 6 degrees of each other for minor aspects.

Planets in Aries		
	oppose	planets in Libra
	square	planets in Cancer and Capricorn
	conjunct	other planets in Aries
	trine	planets in Leo and Sagittarius
	sextile	planets in Gemini and Aquarius
	semi-sextile	planets in Pisces and Taurus
	quincunx	planets in Virgo and Scorpio

Planets in Taurus		
	oppose	planets in Scorpio
	square	planets in Leo and Aquarius
	conjunct	other planets in Taurus
	trine	planets in Virgo and Capricorn
	sextile	planets in Cancer and Pisces
	semi-sextile	planets in Aries and Gemini
	quincunx	planets in Libra and Sagittarius

Planets in Gemini		
	oppose	planets in Sagittarius
	square	planets in Virgo and Pisces
	conjunct	other planets in Gemini
	trine	planets in Libra and Aquarius
	sextile	planets in Aries and Leo
	semi-sextile	planets in Taurus and Cancer
	quincunx	planets in Scorpio and Capricorn

Planets in Cancer		
	oppose	planets in Capricorn
	square	planets in Aries and Libra
	conjunct	other planets in Cancer
	trine	planets in Scorpio and Pisces
	sextile	planets in Taurus and Virgo
	semi-sextile	planets in Gemini and Leo
	quincunx	planets in Sagittarius and Aquarius

Planets in Leo		
	oppose	planets in Aquarius
	square	planets in Taurus and Scorpio
	conjunct	other planets in Leo
	trine	planets in Aries and Sagittarius
	sextile	planets in Gemini and Libra

                semi-sextile ....planets in Cancer and Virgo
                quincunx ....planets in Capricorn and Pisces

Planets in   *oppose* ....planets in Pisces
Virgo   *square* ....planets in Gemini and Sagittarius
                conjunct ....other planets in Virgo
                trine ....planets in Taurus and Capricorn
                sextile ....planets in Cancer and Scorpio
                semi-sextile ....planets in Leo and Libra
                quincunx ....planets in Aries and Aquarius

Planets in   *oppose* ....planets in Aries
Libra   *square* ....planets in Cancer and Capricorn
                conjunct ....other planets in Libra
                trine ....planets in Gemini and Aquarius
                sextile ....planets in Leo and Sagittarius
                semi-sextile ....planets in Virgo and Scorpio
                quincunx ....planets in Taurus and Pisces

Planets in   *oppose* ....planets in Taurus
Scorpio   *square* ....planets in Leo and Aquarius
                conjunct ....other planets in Scorpio
                trine ....planets in Cancer and Pisces
                sextile ....planets in Virgo and Capricorn
                semi-sextile ....planets in Libra and Sagittarius
                quincunx ....planets in Aries and Gemini

Planets in   *oppose* ....planets in Gemini
Sagittarius   *square* ....planets in Virgo and Pisces
                conjunct ....other planets in Sagittarius
                trine ....planets in Aries and Leo
                sextile ....planets in Libra and Aquarius
                semi-sextile ....planets in Scorpio and Capricorn
                quincunx ....planets in Cancer and Taurus

Planets in   *oppose* ....planets in Cancer
Capricorn   *square* ....planets in Aries and Libra

	conjunct	other planets in Capricorn
	trine	planets in Taurus and Virgo
	sextile	planets in Scorpio and Pisces
	semi-sextile	planets in Sagittarius and Aquarius
	quincunx	planets in Gemini and Leo
Planets in	*oppose*	planets in Leo
Aquarius	*square*	planets in Taurus and Scorpio
	conjunct	other planets in Aquarius
	trine	planets in Gemini and Libra
	sextile	planets in Aries and Sagittarius
	semi-sextile	planets in Capricorn and Pisces
	quincunx	planets in Cancer and Virgo
Planets in	*oppose*	planets in Virgo
Pisces	*square*	planets in Gemini and Sagittarius
	conjunct	other planets in Pisces
	trine	planets in Cancer and Scorpio
	sextile	planets in Taurus and Capricorn
	semi-sextile	planets in Aquarius and Aries
	quincunx	planets in Leo and Libra

When you begin interpreting aspects, always bear in mind the challenging aspects are not necessarily damaging. Charts of famous individuals and those of strong characters invariably show tough aspects between planets because these act as a goading mechanism towards achievement. Such a man or woman never gives up and usually follows the old maxim: 'If at first you don't succeed, try, try, try again!'

On the other hand in a generally weak chart, the challenging aspects do give more trouble because the owner of the chart lacks inner strength. In counselling such people, it is vital to boost their confidence by pointing out the positive traits and the positive approach in overcoming obstacles, so that inner strength can be gradually developed.

INTERPRETATION OF ASPECTS

The aspect meanings set out in our lists are condensed for two reasons. Firstly, they are designed to stimulate your own thinking on each aspect as to the blending of one planet's energy with another's. (Never blindly copy out aspects from this list or any textbook.) Consider each one carefully. Apply your own intuitive feeling about how each aspect will fit into the whole personality picture of the completed chart. Secondly, in a simplified course of this nature we cannot go into the complexities of aspect interpretation. You need to read widely and regularly from works by leading authors—many of which are set out in our suggested library list at the end of this course. It is also important to keep up with new overseas research, especially research into the most recently discovered planet, Pluto, if you're aiming for top marks as an analyst.

Remember, too, when you check through the planetary aspect list, that each planet dominates specified personality sectors. For example, the Sun, as the core of being and the true self, always plays a major role. Easy (favourable) aspects to the Sun make the life-force easier to express. Challenging (unfavourable) aspects have obviously the reverse effect. These sectors are outlined below.

To help you identify the planets' influences, in the tables below I have classified the Sun's aspects as markedly affecting everyday life, the Moon's as markedly affecting emotional life, and so on.

The Sun
The Sun symbolizes the true self, the core of being of every individual. Thus any planet aspected by the Sun in a chart will have a more powerful influence. The overall personality and mode of expression will also be modified according to the life principle represented by any planet aspected by the Sun.

The Moon
The Moon symbolizes the inner responses, the instinctive reactions of every individual. Thus any planet aspected by the Moon in a

chart will express its influence in emotional life. Moods, fluctuations in behavioural patterns will be modified by Moon aspects.

Mercury

Mercury symbolizes the mental attitudes and communicative powers of every individual. Thus any planet aspected by Mercury in a chart will express its influence in mental life. Habits of thought, speed in reasoning processes will be modified by Mercury aspects.

Venus

Venus symbolizes the affectional attitudes, the capacity to give and receive love of every individual. Thus any planet aspected by Venus in a chart will express its influence in love-life. Attractions and ability to create harmonious links with others will be modified by Venus aspects.

Mars

Mars symbolizes the physical forces, the sexual energy of every individual. Thus any planet aspected by Mars in a chart will express its influence in physical life. Strength of sexual drives, capacity to provoke reactions in others will be modified by Mars aspects.

Quick-reference data

Natal aspect	Area of influence
Sun	Everyday life
Moon	Emotional life
Mercury	Mental life
Venus	Love-life
Mars	Sex-life

Natal aspects of the Sun—affecting everyday life

Favourables

Sun f. Moon: Focus: will/emotions. Added ease and lack of tension in the expression of the basic life-purpose with greater cohesion in overall personality impact. Harmonizing.

Sun f. Mercury: Focus: will/mind. Added capacity for easy communication and increased mental ability. Intellectualizing.

Sun f. Venus: Focus: will/affections. Added capacity to achieve through personal appeal together with increased artistic and creative interests. Charm-creating.

Sun f. Mars: Focus: will/physical drives. Improved capacity for self-expression, assertiveness, and the use of initiative. Energizing.

Sun f. Jupiter: Focus: will/expansion. Added capacity for successful self-expression and expansion of the scope of activities throughout life, coupled with increased humour and generosity. Broadening.

Sun f. Saturn: Focus: will/discipline. Added capacity for self-control, concentration in pursuit of life-purpose, with more responsible, practical and realistic approach. Disciplining.

Sun f. Uranus: Focus: will/dynamism. Added capacity for independent, unusual and original self-expression with flashes of brilliant insight possible. Magnetizing.

Sun f. Neptune: Focus: will/sublimation. Better capacity for subtlety of expression with marked ability in creative or artistic pursuits. Uplifting.

Sun f. Pluto: Focus: will/regeneration. Good rapport between the will and the subconscious drives, increasing inner strength and ability to command others. Eliminating.

Unfavourables

Sun u. Moon: Focus: will/emotions. Clash between the ego demand and emotional needs thereby producing uncertainty, restlessness and a recurring sense of inner frustration. Disturbing.

Sun u. Mercury and Venus: No major disharmonious aspects can occur as these planets are never far enough apart.

Sun u. Mars: Focus: will/physical drives. Tendency towards over-reaction, waste of physical forces and over-impulsive behaviour. Depleting.

Sun u. Jupiter: Focus: will/expansion. Likelihood of problems caused by over-expectations of others and tendency towards periods of bad judgement, exaggeration and extravagance. Over-doing.

Sun u. Saturn: Focus: will/discipline. Tendency towards deep-rooted inhibitions, over-caution and a tendency to take a narrow approach on occasions. Depressing.

Sun u. Uranus: Focus: will/dynamism. Tendency towards erratic, rebellious, self-willed behavioural patterns at times caused by impatience and the demand for total personal freedom. Damaging.

Sun u. Neptune: Focus: will/sublimation. Periods of escapist behaviour with tendency to self-deception and avoidance of the facts of situations or events. Deluding.

Sun u. Pluto: Focus: will/regeneration. Extreme behaviour plus clash between the will and the subconscious drives, thereby causing great difficulty in realizing and expressing needs of the self. Overbearing.

Natal aspects of the Moon—affecting emotional life

Favourables

Moon f. Sun: See Moon under Natal Aspects of the Sun.

Moon f. Mercury: Focus: emotions/mind. Better capacity to verbalize emotions to ensure better understanding with others. Communicating.

Moon f. Venus: Focus: emotions/affections. Added responsiveness, harmony and ease in emotional reactions. Pleasing.

Moon f. Mars: Focus: emotions/physical drives. Added capacity for energetic and swift response but with better self-control and discretion in the expression of emotions. Warming.

Moon f. Jupiter: Focus: emotions/expansion. Better capacity for geniality and instinctive good judgement in love relationships. Open-hearted.

Moon f. Saturn: Focus: emotions/discipline. Added ability for self-discipline and caution in emotional reactions, although some inhibitions possible. Supportive.

Moon f. Uranus: Focus: emotions/dynamism. Added ability for purposeful, progressive changes in emotional life, coupled with increased personal charisma. Dynamic.

Moon f. Neptune: Focus: emotions/sublimation. Much greater sensitivity, gentleness and subtlety in all emotional responses, coupled with the ability to apply imagination and understanding. Refining.

Moon f. Pluto: Focus: emotions/regeneration. Good rapport between the emotions and the subconscious drives, thereby making all emotional relationships in life easier to handle. Penetrative.

Unfavourables

Moon u. Sun: See Moon under Natal Aspects of the Sun.

Moon u. Mercury: Focus: emotions/mind. Difficulty in verbalizing the emotions and expressing them easily so that misunderstandings are always possible. Blocking.

Moon u. Venus: Focus: emotions/affections. Clash between the emotional expression and the display of love and affection, coupled with awkwardness in expressing feelings. Discomforting.

Moon u. Mars: Focus: emotions/physical drives. Tendency towards highly intolerant, impulsive and over-forceful reactions in emotional situations. Disconcerting.

Moon u. Jupiter: Focus: emotions/expansion. Tendency towards over-responsiveness, extravagant and unstable emotional reactions producing difficulties and misunderstandings. Wasteful.

Moon u. Saturn: Focus: emotions/discipline. Tendency towards over-sensitivity in emotional life with over-control or repression of responses. Narrowing.

Moon u. Uranus: Focus: emotions/dynamism. Tendency towards self-willed, over-excitable and erratic reactions in emotional situations. Rebellious.

Moon u. Neptune: Focus: emotions/sublimation. Likelihood of confused and chaotic situations at times in all emotional relationships and tendency towards ignoring problems or running away from them. Evasive.

Moon u. Pluto: Focus: emotions/regeneration. Tendency towards over-demand in emotional affairs, extremist behaviour and fear of responsibility. Destructive.

Natal aspects of Mercury—affecting mental life

Favourables

Sun: See under Natal Aspects of the Sun.

Moon: See under Natal Aspects of the Moon.

Mercury f. Venus: Focus: mind/affections. Added capacity for pleasantness and ease in the way opinions and ideas are communicated. Expressive.

Mercury f. Mars: Focus: mind/physical drives. Added capacity for fast, forceful mental reactions coupled with constructive thinking and an enterprising approach. Responsive.

Mercury f. Jupiter: Focus: mind/expansion. Added capacity for mental optimism plus wider dimensions of thought in all forms of intellectual pursuits. Developing.

Mercury f. Saturn: Focus: mind/discipline. Added capacity for disciplined, concentrated thinking with good powers of logical deduction. Reasoning.

Mercury f. Uranus: Focus: mind/dynamism. Likelihood of highly original, innovative and perceptive forms of thinking. Inventive.

Mercury f. Neptune: Focus: mind/sublimation. Added subtlety, imagination and use of intuition in all forms of communication. Sensitizing.

Mercury f. Pluto: Focus: mind/regeneration. Improved capacity for investigative thinking and for reliance on subconscious promptings and instinctual reasoning. Intuitive.

Unfavourables

Sun: See Mercury under Natal Aspects of the Sun.

Moon: See Mercury under Natal Aspects of the Moon.

Mercury u. Venus: No major disharmonious aspects can occur between Mercury and Venus as they are never more than 76 degrees apart.

Mercury u. Mars: Focus: mind/physical drives. Likelihood of overly fast reactions at times with argumentativeness and caustic comment likely. Harsh.

Mercury u. Jupiter: Focus: mind/expansion. Likely to suffer from periods of careless judgement in mental activities, over-expectation of others and sometimes overblown ideas. Exaggerating.

Mercury u. Saturn: Focus: mind/discipline. Difficulty in stimulating a sense of confidence in all areas of mental activity, lack of objectivity on occasions. Restricting.

Mercury u. Uranus: Focus: mind/dynamism. Tendency towards extremist ideas, high impatience and irritation if others do not grasp the original and inventive ideas of the self. Overly radical.

Mercury u. Neptune: Focus: mind/sublimation. Possibility of periods of confused thinking and self-deception, coupled with escapist tendencies when forced to face facts. Delusive.

Mercury u. Pluto: Focus: mind/regeneration. Tendency towards periods of extremely depressive thinking, coupled with needless worries and fears which can become obsessive. Gloomy.

Natal aspects of Venus—affecting love-life and affections

Favourables

Sun: See Venus under Natal Aspects of the Sun.

Moon: See Venus under Natal Aspects of the Moon.

Mercury: See Venus under Natal Aspects of Mercury.

Venus f. Mars: Focus: affections/physical drives. Better capacity for warm responses in love relationships, coupled with increased sensuality. Pleasing.

Venus f. Jupiter: Focus: affections/expansion. Added capacity for charm, easy popularity and generous responses, coupled with expansiveness and warmth. Brightening.

Venus f. Saturn: Focus: affections/discipline. Added capacity for serious, practical behaviour in affectional situations, coupled with strong sense of propriety. Responsible.

Venus f. Uranus: Focus: affections/dynamism. Likelihood of very unusual tastes, unconventional values and attraction to off-beat types in affectional relationships. Electric.

Venus f. Neptune: Focus: affections/sublimation. Added capacity for subtlety and idealism in the expression of love and affection, coupled with marked sentimentality. Comforting.

Venus f. Pluto: Focus: affections/regeneration. Better capacity to attract others easily and greater likelihood of choosing correct type of life partner. Intensifying.

Unfavourables

Sun: See Venus under Natal Aspects of the Sun.

Moon: See Venus under Natal Aspects of the Moon.

Mercury: See Venus under Natal Aspects of Mercury.

Venus u. Mars: Focus: affections/physical drives. Tendency towards over-forcefulness, periods of discontent and difficulty in personal relationships. Demanding.

Venus u. Jupiter: Focus: affections/expansion. Possibility of over-reaction and extravagant reactions and at times over-expectation of those loved. Swamping.

Venus u. Saturn: Focus: affections/discipline. Tendency to set very high and exacting standards for those cared about so that affection becomes very difficult to express. Rejecting.

Venus u. Uranus: Focus: affections/dynamism. Likelihood of marked personal magnetism with attraction to unusual, unorthodox types in affectional relationships. Disconcerting.

Venus u. Neptune: Focus: affections/sublimation. Likelihood of inability to face facts in affectional relationships and a tendency to take escapist answers when baulked or thwarted. Fantasizing.

Venus u. Pluto: Focus: affections/regeneration. Tendency towards overdoing attempts to attract others, thus creating personal life unpheavals, hurtful breaks in close relationships and inability to co-operate with those loved. Damaging.

Natal aspects of Mars—affecting sex-life and physical activities

Favourables

Sun: See Mars under Natal Aspects of the Sun.

Moon: See Mars under Natal Aspects of the Moon.

Mercury: See Mars under Natal Aspects of Mercury.

Venus: See Mars under Natal Aspects of Venus.

Mars f. Jupiter: Focus: physical drives/expansion. Improved enthusiasm, adventurousness and uninhibited behaviour, coupled with outgoing responses. Generous.

Mars f. Saturn: Focus: physical drives/discipline. Improved capacity for supportiveness and reliability, coupled with control of physical desires. Strengthening.

Mars f. Uranus: Focus: physical drives/dynamism. Added capacity for energy, excitement and impulsive behaviour in physical responses which exerts a magnetic appeal for others. Spontaneous.

Mars f. Neptune: Focus: physical drives/sublimation. Added capacity for subtlety, sensitivity and understanding of the needs of the sex partner. Deepening.

Mars f. Pluto: Focus: physical drives/regeneration. Good rapport between the will and the subconscious drives thereby permitting easier release of excess energy, either of a sexual or physical nature. Powerful.

Unfavourables

Sun: See Mars under Natal Aspects of the Sun.

Moon: See Mars under Natal Aspects of the Moon.

Mercury: See Mars under Natal Aspects of Mercury.

Venus: See Mars under Natal Aspects of Venus.

Mars u. Jupiter: Focus: physical drives/expansion. Tendency towards over-statement, over-give and periods of over-enthusiasm in all areas of physical activity. Off-putting.

Mars u. Saturn: Focus: physical drives/discipline. Risk of alienation of the sex partner and the setting of severe, narrowing standards in behaviour. Austere.

Mars u. Uranus: Focus: physical drives/dynamism. Likelihood of very irritable and over-intense reactions on occasions, coupled with extreme self-will. High-handed.

Mars u. Neptune: Focus: physical drives/sublimation. Tendency towards evading the clear-cut issues of any physical confrontation. Unreal.

Mars u. Pluto: Focus: physical drives/regeneration. Tendency towards obsessive and over-intense reactions caused by repression of sexual or physical energies. Domineering.

DO's AND DON'Ts IN ASPECT INTERPRETATION

Now for a short run-through on the 'do's' and 'don'ts' when you begin to analyse planetary aspects.

Don't over-emphasize any one aspect. The chart must always be viewed as a whole, so all the aspects must be woven together.

Do check exact and wide aspects. The closer the degree of an aspect between two planets, the more intense its effect.

Don't ignore unaspected planets. Any planet without major aspects shows a lack of channelling of the energy of that planet (e.g., an unaspected Mars in a chart suggests that the individual will strike problems in directing both the physical forces and sex drives).

Do give added significance to any aspect if one of the planets making such aspect is the ruler of the Ascendant or the Sun. (Rulers were set out in Chapter 1. Refer back if you can't remember them all.)

TEXT EXERCISES

Note
In Volume 3 of his 12-volume treatise, *The Principles and Practice of Astrology*, American psychologist/astrologer Noel Tyl provides capsule comments on major planetary aspects. In her major work, *The Modern Textbook of Astrology*, renowned British astrologer Margaret Hone does the same.

   The following set of questions covers excerpts from interpretations of major planetary aspects by these two leading authors. A study of these will also show you the slightly differing emphasis given to each aspect by each writer.

   The abbreviation F denotes a favourable aspect, U an unfavourable one.

1. *Aspects of the Sun*
State in your opinion which type of aspect is referred to and which

planet is aspecting the Sun in the following statements by Tyl and Hone (e.g., Sun F Venus). Give the reasons for your choice in each case.

(a) 'Good luck, magnanimity, largesse, pride, indulgence, enthusiasm.' (Tyl)

(b) 'Separations. Temperament. Wild beginnings. Intellectual development ahead of emotional development. Independence. Liberalism. Self is right; the world is wrong.' (Tyl)

(c) 'Abundant physical vitality. Leadership. Tireless force.' (Tyl)

(d) 'Severity. Great sense of responsibility. Worry, anxiety, delay.' (Tyl)

(e) 'Tendency to overstrain through overdoing, thus impairing the vitality. Pugnacious and bad tempered.' (Hone)

(f) 'Independent, interesting, dramatic, tendency to scientific thought. Rebellious. Original.' (Hone)

(g) 'Tendency to advance the self through ruthless behaviour to others.' (Hone)

(h) 'Self-expression is through the affections, through beauty and art and gentle ways.' (Hone)

2. *Aspects of the Moon*

State in your opinion which type of aspect is referred to and which planet is aspecting the Moon in the following statements by Tyl and Hone (e.g., Moon U Pluto). Give your reasons for choice in each case.

(a) 'Overcompensation. A demand for success. For women: a charm and magnetism with men.' (Tyl)

(b) 'Articulate, expressive, witty. Persistence and depth needed.' (Tyl)

(c) 'Gracefulness, intuition. Beauty in all forms has a strong effect upon the Self. Peace and quiet. Subjective comfort.' (Tyl)

(d) 'Emotions and popularity can need reassurance. Aloneness avoids risk of exposure. Aesthetic awareness.' (Tyl)

(e) 'Uneasy expression of the affections and lack of harmony in the home.' (Hone)

(f) 'Excellent strength physically and emotionally. Ability to work and push on in life.' (Hone)

(g) 'Greater sensitivity. Tendency to retirement and philanthropy and to day-dreaming.' (Hone)

(h) 'The sense of lack intensifies the shyness and prevents easy response to what could bring happiness. Relations with women and mother not easy. The practical is over-valued. Tendency to meet hardships.' (Hone)

3. *Aspects of Mercury*

State in your opinion which type of aspect is referred to and which planet is aspecting Mercury in the following statements by Tyl and Hone (e.g., Mercury F Venus). Give the reasons for your choice.

(a) 'Depression, melancholy. Sensitivity to shallowness and the superficial creates feelings of frustration along the path to personal wisdom, Subtlety is appreciated. Mental cruelty is possible.' (Tyl)

(b) 'Absorbed in the hidden, the occult, the underworld, the underground. Tendency to an awareness of individual futility. Morbidity.' (Tyl)

(c) 'Quick mind, facility. Possible waste of these easy energies.' (Tyl)

(d) 'Exaggeration needs adjustment through objectivity.' (Tyl)

(e) 'The mind and the mental outlook are improved in so far as charm of speech, pleasantness of manner are concerned. But ease rather than strength is gained.' (Hone)

(f) 'The mind and nervous system can now be energized to the point of being overstrained. Irritability and temper. Incisiveness becomes satirical and carping.' (Hone)

(g) 'A cheerful, humorous witty mentality and success through its exercise.' (Hone)

(h) 'Order now becomes rigid discipline and dreary planning. Lack of poise forces brusque speech and writing.' (Hone)

4. *Aspects of Venus*

State in your opinion which type of aspect is referred to and which planet is aspecting Venus in the following statements by Tyl and Hone (e.g., Venus F Mars). Give the reasons for your choice in each case.

(a) 'Extreme attraction to and for the opposite sex. Luck and charisma.' (Tyl)

(b) 'The emotions and passions are given tension. Sex and love can present problems. Misdirected affections. Blind love.' (Tyl)

(c) 'Nervous tension over the unusual, the innovative, with regard to emotions, sex and friendships. Temperamental.' (Tyl)

(d) 'Emotional viewpoint is broadest. Understanding is deep and rejuvenating.' (Tyl)

(e) 'Warmth and enthusiasm enter into relationships of affection, both in sexual life and as expressed to young people in a family.' (Hone)

(f) 'Partnerships are unconventional and apt to be broken because of insistence on freedom. Partings are likely through unhappy causes.' (Hone)

(g) 'Affections and partnerships subject to disclosures and upheavals and new starts.' (Hone)

(h) 'Affection most difficult to express. Life tends to be solitary. Any partnership brings responsibility. Sorrow or loss through affections.' (Hone)

5. *Aspects of Mars*

State in your opinion which type of aspect is referred to and which planet is aspecting Mars in the following statements by Tyl and Hone (e.g., Mars U Pluto). Give the reasons for your choice in each case.

(a) 'Energy, flair, enthusiasm, creativity, *joie de vivre*.' (Tyl)

(b) 'The most powerful magnetic aspect in any horoscope: the energies of Mars are given an intuitive, aesthetic delivery.' (Tyl)

(c) 'Strategy. Building carefully from solid foundations. Boldness complements caution.' (Tyl)

(d) 'Energies cannot tune in with proper application.' (Tyl)

(e) 'Energy is vastly increased. Desire for enjoyment and widespread activity of mind and body is keen. Daring, courage and argumentativeness are increased.' (Hone)

(f) 'Ability to love and to enjoy sexual life and things of beauty is strengthened and made more robust but less delicate.' (Hone)

(g) 'Explosive temper and wilful impatience and nervous strain do not make for easy partnership in marriage or business. Breaks of personal relationships occur.' (Hone)

(h) 'Vivid over-imagination without commonsense produces

chaos. Irregular, over-glamorous, escapist ways bring downfall.'
(Hone)

MODEL ANSWERS

Note
The model answers given in the following pages are offered in fairly
brief outline as guidance to each test participant. Your own answers
do not have to be exactly the same to be marked as correct. Original
thinking is always rewarded, provided that your ideas show you
have learned and understood the basic tenets of astrological theory.

1. *Aspects of the Sun*
(a) Sun conjunct Jupiter: favourable. The ego thrust of the Sun
     gains expansiveness and opportunity from the broadening
     energy of Jupiter.
(b) Sun square Uranus: unfavourable. The ego thrust of the Sun
     is diverted, made erratic by the disruptive energy of Uranus.
(c) Sun trine Mars: favourable. The ego thrust of the Sun is boosted
     by the fiery energy of Mars.
(d) Sun opposition Saturn: unfavourable. The ego thrust of the
     Sun is overwhelmed by the inhibitive energy of Saturn.
(e) Sun square or opposition Mars: unfavourable. The ego thrust
     of the Sun is over-boosted by the aggressive energy of Mars.
(f) Sun conjunct Uranus: partially favourable. The ego thrust of
     the Sun is electrified by the magnetic energy of Uranus.
(g) Sun square or opposition Pluto: unfavourable. The ego thrust
     of the Sun is hardened by the ruthless energy of Pluto.
(h) Sun conjunct Venus: favourable. The ego thrust of the Sun
     is softened by the calming energy of Venus.

2. *Aspects of the Moon*
(a) Moon conjunct Mars: partially favourable. The emotional need
     of the Moon is made overly demanding by the fiery energy
     of Mars.
(b) Moon square Mercury: partially favourable. The emotional
     need of the Moon is overly verbalized by the intellectual energy
     of Mercury.

(c) Moon trine Neptune: favourable. The emotional need of the Moon is given depth by the spiritual energy of Neptune.

(d) Moon opposition Venus: unfavourable. The emotional need of the Moon is made vacillating by the languid energy of Venus.

(e) Moon square or opposition Venus: unfavourable, exhibiting in similar manner to (d).

(f) Moon trine Mars: favourable. The emotional need of the Moon is given vigorous expression by the vital energy of Mars.

(g) Moon conjunct Neptune: partially favourable. The emotional needs of the Moon is sensitized by the subtle energy of Neptune.

(h) Moon square or opposition Saturn: unfavourable. The emotional need of the Moon is chilled by rejecting energy of Saturn.

3. *Aspects of Mercury*

(a) Mercury square Saturn: unfavourable. The mental thrust of Mercury is bogged down by the heavy energy of Saturn.

(b) Mercury conjunct Pluto: partially unfavourable. The mental thrust of Mercury is pulled down into the subconscious by the compulsive energy of Pluto.

(c) Mercury conjunct Mars: partially favourable. The mental thrust of Mercury is pushed into overdrive by the impatient energy of Mars.

(d) Mercury opposition Jupiter: unfavourable. The mental thrust of Mercury is spread too broadly by the expansive energy of Jupiter.

(e) Mercury conjunct Venus: partially favourable. The mental thrust of Mercury is made more pleasingly expressive by the smoothing energy of Venus.

(f) Mercury square or opposition Mars: unfavourable. The mental thrust of Mercury is made overly direct by the combative energy of Mars.

(g) Mercury trine Jupiter: favourable. The mental thrust of Mercury is brightened by outgoing energy of Jupiter.

(h) Mercury square or opposition Saturn: unfavourable. The mental thrust of Mercury is drawn down into pessimism by the blocking energy of Saturn.

4. *Aspects of Venus*

(a) Venus conjunct Mars: favourable. Venus' search for love is energized by the physical energy of Mars.

(b) Venus square Mars: unfavourable. Venus' search for love is overstressed by the sexual energy of Mars.

(c) Venus opposition Uranus: unfavourable. Venus' search for love is made erratic by the eccentric energy of Uranus.

(d) Venus trine Pluto: favourable. Venus' search for love is given depth by the intensifying energy of Pluto.

(e) Venus trine Mars: favourable. Venus' search for love is made more all-embracing by the positive energy of Mars.

(f) Venus square or opposition Uranus: unfavourable. Venus' search for love exhibits as in (c).

(g) Venus conjunct Pluto: partially favourable. Venus' search for love is drawn down into the subconscious by the compulsive energy of Pluto.

(h) Venus square or opposition Saturn: unfavourable. Venus' search for love is forced into repression by the constricting energy of Saturn.

5. *Aspects of Mars*

(a) Mars conjunct Jupiter: favourable. The drive for physical satisfaction of Mars is uplifted by the exhilarating energy of Jupiter.

(b) Mars conjunct Neptune: favourable. The drive for physical satisfaction of Mars is made virtually magical by the intuitive energy of Neptune.

(c) Mars trine Saturn: favourable. The drive for physical satisfaction is given solidarity by the supportive energy of Saturn.

(d) Mars opposition Pluto: unfavourable. The drive for physical satisfaction of Mars wastes itself against the obstructive energy of Pluto.

(e) Mars conjunct Jupiter: favourable. The drive for physical satisfaction is made less self-oriented by the hearty energy of Jupiter.

(f) Mars conjunct Venus: favourable. The drive for physical

satisfaction of Mars is softened by the gentler energies of Venus.

(g) Mars square or opposition Uranus: unfavourable. The drive for physical satisfaction of Mars loses sensitivity through the disruptive energy of Uranus.

(h) Mars square or opposition Neptune: unfavourable. The drive for physical satisfaction loses clarity through the deceptive energy of Neptune.

Southern Hemisphere birth example

Cardinal signs 3
Fixed signs 4
Mutable signs 3
Positive signs 2
Negative signs 8

Name: John Jones

G. 1.40 a.m.
B. Sydney, Australia
S. Placidean

FIRE signs 1
AIR signs 1
EARTH signs 4
WATER signs 4

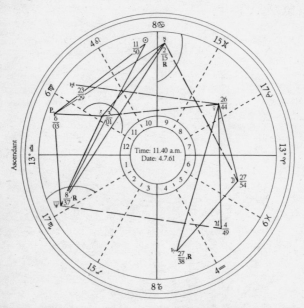

B.T.Q.	Planet	Natal	Major Aspects
N F W	1♆ Neptune	8.37♏ R	✶ ♇
P F F	11♅ Uranus	23.29♌	
N C E	4♄ Saturn	27.38♑ R	
P F A	5♃ Jupiter	4.49♒ R	□ ♆
N M E	11♂ Mars	3.01♍	♂ ♇ ✶ ♆
N C W	10☉ Sun	11.50♋	✶ ♇ △ ♆
N F E	8♀ Venus	26.44♉	□ ♂ △ ♃ △ ♄ □ ♅
N C W	9☿ Mercury	2.15♋ R	✶ ♇ ✶ ♂ △ ♆
N M W	6☽ Moon	27.54♓	□ ☿ ✶ ♀ ✶ ♄
N M E	12♇ Pluto	6.03♍	

Northern Hemisphere birth example

Cardinal signs 5
Fixed signs 3
Mutable signs 2
Positive signs 7
Negative signs 3

Name: Jean Smith

G. 6.10 p.m.
B. Ruse, Bulgaria
S. Placidean

FIRE signs 2
AIR signs 5
EARTH signs 1
WATER signs 2

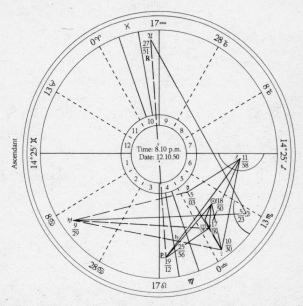

B.T.Q.	Planet	Natal	Major Aspects
P C A	5 ♆ Neptune	17.11 ♎	⚹ ♇
N C W	2 ♅ Uranus	9.29 ♋	□ ♆
N M E	4 ♄ Saturn	25.56 ♏	
P F A	10 ♃ Jupiter	27.51 ♒ R	☍ ♇
P M F	7 ♂ Mars	11.58 ♐	△ ♇ ⚹ ♆
P C A	5 ☉ Sun	18.50 ♎	⚹ ♇ ♂ ♀ ♂ ♆
P C A	5 ♀ Venus	10.38 ♎	⚹ ☍ □ ♅ ♂ ♆
P C A	5 ☿ Mercury	5.03 ♎	♂ ♀ ⚹ ☍ □ ♅
N F W	5 ☽ Moon	5.23 ♏	△ ♃ △ ♅
P F F	4 ♇ Pluto	19.12 ♌	

5.

CHART ERECTION

TIMING

If mathematics of any kind makes you break out in a cold sweat, this section is where the going appears to be getting really rough! We say 'appears' because basic astrological calculations are nothing like as mind-blowing as they look at first glance.

It is true that mistakes in calculation can be devastating, causing a kind of chain-reaction of error, but they only happen if the fundamental concepts are not thoroughly understood at the outset.

Hence I've tried to ensure you don't misunderstand or forget any vital step—by including birth computation sheets that are as close to mistake-proof as I can make them. I've also endeavoured to anticipate and prevent any problem patches bogging you down in this section by stating the rules as plainly as possible and only adding the explanations for their existence where necessary.

Don't despair and down tools if you don't get your calculations right straight away. Few novices do! I've never quite forgotten how I gnashed my teeth, bit my fingernails to the quicks, and hurled the whole tangled mess into the waste-paper basket, when I first tackled astrological maths way back in the 1960s.

Like thousands of others, I had tried to learn astrology from various textbooks but found so many leading authors seemed to assume their readers were all naturally expert in mathematics, geography and astronomy (which I definitely wasn't!). Worse still, I discovered one author propounded one method and approach, while another came up with something quite different, thereby making the tangle even knottier.

Hence, in this short course, I have tried to recall and explain all the tricky bits that once threw me—to convince you that astrological maths is *not* difficult, just pernickety! And I have tried to ensure that you don't cut corners and thus make confidence-destroying mistakes.

Remember at all times in astrological calculation, we are dealing with units of time—i.e., hours, minutes and seconds. Thus you cannot use ordinary calculators for this work as they use decimals—i.e., units of ten.

There are, as we all know, 60 minutes in one hour, 60 seconds in one minute. Thus when we calculate we add or subtract in these time units.

The three kinds of time

1. Standard or zone time
This type of time is the precise time shown on clocks in any given country at any given birth. Sometimes this will vary within a country from one state, county or province to another. Sometimes, especially in smaller countries, the zone or standard time is the same throughout that country.

We will list the standard or zone times for Australia and New Zealand hereunder. For other countries, you need to check in appropriate reference works.

Margaret Hone's comprehensive book, *The Modern Textbook of Astrology*, contains a list of standard times in many countries of the world in Appendix 2, page 307 (1972 edn.). Also, Doris Chase Doane's, *Time Changes in the World*, gives standard times for the world. She has published three books including a separate one for the USA and another for Canada and Mexico. Her books also give data on daylight saving time applicable in all countries.

Take extra special care when working on USA births. American time zones and daylight saving periods vary enormously!

Solar system: relative sizes of planets and order from sun

Distances from Sun and the time of journey for light to travel from the Sun to the respective planets, are also indicated below. As light travels at the rate of about 299,300km (186,000 miles) per second (!!), it can be understood what fantastic distances are involved. However, all the planets are comparatively close when one considers that outside the solar system, the nearest heavenly body is about 4½ years light-travel away.

SUN	Mercury	Venus	Earth	Mars	Jupiter	Saturn	Uranus	Neptune	Pluto
Distance from Sun (in millions)									
kilometres:	58	108	150	227	649	1426	2868	4495	5793
miles:	36	67	93	141	483	886	1782	2793	3600
Time of travel of light from Sun to planet:	3m.14s	6m	8m.20s	12½m	43m.16s	1h.19m	2h.40m	4h.10m	5½h

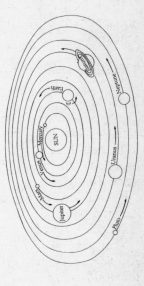

Standard or zone times for Australia

East Coast (Queensland to Tasmania)	= 150 degrees 00 minutes *East*
South Australia (+Northern Territory and Broken Hill)	= 142 degrees 30 minutes *East*
Western Australia	= 120 degrees 00 minutes *East*

Standard or zone times for New Zealand

Prior to 1 January 1946	= 172 degrees 30 minutes *East*
From 1 January 1946	= 180 degrees 00 minutes *East*

You'll appreciate better the importance of standard times in calculation when we begin to erect a sample chart, but for now just note the Australian and New Zealand data carefully.

2. *Greenwich Mean Time*

If you've studied astrology books before, you'll have observed the initials GMT appearing on sample charts. This is, of course, the abbreviation for Greenwich Mean Time. It is also the standard or zone time used in Britain.

When you check through the ephemeris (Planetary Tables) note if the book you're using is set up for the planets' positions at a *noon* GMT or a *midnight* GMT. This information is always stated in the front of any ephemeris.

For individuals born in Britain, the birthtime will be within the zone of Greenwich Mean Time so no conversion is needed. For individuals born outside Britain, the birthtime will be within the time zone of the birthplace. For example, for a birth in Manchester, England, '0 hours 00 minutes' is written on your Birth Calculation Sheet on the Zone Standard line. (Check now the sample sheet on this section.)

For a birth in Sydney, Australia, '10 hours 00 minutes' is written on your Birth Calculation Sheet on the Zone or Standard line, because the zone time of Eastern Australia is 10 hours *ahead* of Greenwich Mean Time. So 10 hours must be *subtracted* to obtain the correct GMT.

Don't worry if all this sounds somewhat confusing at this stage.

Once you apply time data in chart erection, you'll discover it is far easier to understand than it sounds right now.

The term 'mean' needs a little further elaboration, too. It adds up to nothing more than its dictionary description: 'average'. You'll find the term used when 'Greenwich Mean Time' or 'Local Mean Time' are mentioned in astrological texts. Why? Civilized life relies on the use of clocks which move uniformly through the hours of each day. But the earth itself does not move uniformly in its daily orbit as you'll see if you inspect a sundial. The sundial shows the *true* local time indicated by the sun's position at any hour: the clocks show the uniform mean (or average) time in any country for any hour. The Local Mean Time is, naturally, the kind of time we refer to when we consider local time at a birth.

3. Clock time at birth

This is usually the time stated to you as the moment of birth. A few countries (happily) state it on birth certificates, but most (unhappily) do not. Some people have hospital cards showing birthtime, however, and many major maternity hospitals keep records. Some will give this information free of charge, others require a substantial fee to search their records.

If an individual does not know their birthtime and no accurate record of it remains, do not attempt to erect a chart for him/her until you have become a fully qualified and experienced astrologer.

'Rectification' of birthtime is a very complex process, full of traps, and far beyond the scope of beginners in astrological study. The term itself briefly means locating birthtime from past experiences in the life of a given individual and the planetary birth patterns implied by such experiences.

When discussing birthtime, check your enquirer's source of information. Accuracy on this point is vital. Some people deduct daylight saving time when giving their birth data. Most do not, but this must be double-checked.

Clock time at birth, then, is the standard time in the country on the date where the birth occurred.

Daylight saving time (also known as summer time)
This practice of putting clocks forward to make better use of daylight hours during summer dates back to World War One and has been used intermittently in many countries ever since. In most cases, daylight saving time requires all clocks in a given country, state or province to be *advanced one hour* at a specific time on a specific date during summer. However, there were also some periods in certain countries during and shortly after World War Two when daylight saving applied continuously all through winter as well. There were also certain periods when 'double summer time', i.e., *clocks to be advanced two hours* applied.

In a concise course of this nature, we cannot include all these lengthy daylight saving time lists. But you will find them comprehensively set out in Doris Chase Doane's *Time Changes in the World*. Also, most major public libraries have this information.

Never forget to check for daylight saving time when erecting any chart. If you miss this detail, all your calculations will be incorrect.

Remember, too, daylight saving time is, in reality, 'artificial' time. For example, an individual born at 7.23 a.m. during a one-hour daylight saving time period was *actually* born at 6.23 a.m. So 6.23 a.m. must be treated as the real birthtime when calculating.

Sidereal time
Just before we move on to the calculations required for the *place* of birth, there are two more pointers on the matter of time, the first requiring the understanding of the term 'sidereal time'. In your planetary ephemeris, you'll find this shown in a specific column which will be printed something like this:

July 1961

D		S.T.	
	H	M	S
4	6	49	02

D = Date. Here 4.7.61

S.T.   = Sidereal time
H.M.S = Hours, Minutes, Seconds of Sidereal Time

Thus S.T. on 4 July 1961 = 6 hours 49 minutes 2 seconds.

Remember, all our calculations are done by using a *noon ephemeris*. Your data will be different if you try to work with a *midnight ephemeris*, so don't confuse yourself by attempting this. (Whether calculations are printed as at noon or midnight is always stated in the ephemeris book. Be sure to check.)

We won't include the full technical definition of the word 'sidereal' here, but it will help your understanding if you simply note the word derives from the Latin word for 'star'. Hence, 'sidereal' time means 'star' time.

Acceleration on time interval

This is yet another minor adjustment in time that has to be calculated and placed in the appropriate slot on your Birth Calculation Sheet. The term 'interval' refers to the interval (or period) *to* or *from* noon of the birthtime, using a noon ephemeris. For example: an 11 a.m. birth shows an interval *to* noon of one hour; a 7 p.m. birth shows an interval *from* noon of seven hours.

The term 'acceleration' represents a correction for sidereal time at the rate of *10 seconds for every hour.*

Thus the 11 a.m. birthtime requires a minus adjustment of 10 seconds, as there is only one hour between 11 a.m. and the subsequent noon. And the 7 p.m. birthtime requires a plus adjustment of 70 seconds—i.e., 1 minute 10 seconds, as there are seven hours between 7 p.m. and the preceding noon.

Spot check: a very common mistake with beginners when they're calculating a.m. time intervals either with GMT or acceleration, is to overlook that it is a subtraction of *the difference* in hours and minutes from noon (using noon ephemeris of course), not the hours and minutes as stated. For example, the time of 7.47 a.m. is separated from the subsequent noon by an interval of 4 hours 13 minutes. But some students tend to subtract 7 hours 47 minutes by mistake.

LOCATION

The next question we have to tackle is precisely where a given birth occurred, and that means a short sortie into the world of geography.

If you closed your atlas for the last time when you left primary school, you'll need to buy yourself a new one now to reactivate the memory banks and retrieve that long-lost knowledge. If you're a geography buff, please accept the fact that we must include the following basic definitions because a general grasp of longitude, latitude, etc., is very important in astrological calculation. So let's open our atlas now. In the back of any good recent edition, you'll find an index of the longitude and latitude of all major towns and cities in the world.

Note first that *longitude* is always measured geographically east or west from the meridian of Greenwich Observatory in England; *latitude* is always measured geographically north or south of the Equator. (It is the Equator which divides the Northern and Southern Hemispheres of the globe.)

Longitude calculation

For any birthplace other than one occurring on the Greenwich meridian, you must make the necessary adjustment for the difference in longitude.

You obtain the adjustment figure easily by multiplying the degrees and minutes of the longitude of the birthplace by 4.

After the multiplication is made, the result is added to your Birth Calculation Sheet in the appropriate slot, as hours, minutes and seconds of time. (This adjustment is based on the Earth's rotation of 360 degrees every twenty-four hours, breaking down to one degree every four minutes.)

To illustrate longitude:
Take a birth occurring in Kingston, Jamaica.

Latitude of Jamaica = 18 degrees 00 minutes north; longitude of Jamaica = 76 degrees 52 minutes west. (These figures are shown in all good atlases.)

To calculate longitude for Jamaica, we thus multiply 76 degrees 52 minutes by 4, remembering we are dealing with units of time, not decimal units.

Result of this sum = 5 hours 07 minutes 28 seconds, because the degrees and minutes of longitude are treated in astrology as hours, minutes and seconds of time.

In case you're still a trifle puzzled, let's take the sum apart, step by step.

1. Our first multiplication by 4 of 76 degrees 52 minutes gives a result of 304 minutes and 208 seconds.

2. Those 208 seconds convert to 3 minutes 28 seconds because there are 60 seconds in every minute.

3. These 3 minutes are added to the original 304 minutes, thus equalling 307 minutes. There are 60 minutes in every hour so now our 307 minutes converts to 5 hours 7 minutes plus the 28 seconds.

4. As Jamaica is *west* of Greenwich the above figure is *subtracted* on the longitude line in our birth calculation sheet.

Never forget whenever you're handling a birth which occurred in a longitude *east* of Greenwich, you must *add* the longitude adjustment *figure* in the appropriate slot on your Birth Calculation Sheet. Whenever you're handling a birth which occurred in a longitude *west* of Greenwich, you must *subtract* the longitude adjustment figure in the appropriate slot on your Birth Calculation Sheet.

Be very careful with this! Many novices slip up by entering minutes in the hours column on the sheet or the other way round; or by multiplying latitude degrees instead of longitude.

Latitude is much easier to check. You simply take the nearest degree of latitude to the birthplace from the appropriate page of the Tables of Houses.

Tables of houses
There are quite a few different books of Houses Tables available and if you're planning to erect charts yourself you'll need to buy

your House Tables before you can begin.

Many practitioners use the Koch House Tables, including myself. This is a small book, printed in Germany but obtainable from all bookshops specializing in astrological texts. It is designed for Northern Hemisphere births but, as you'll see with our sample chart calculations, the data can be applied in the manner shown later for Southern Hemisphere births.

In the Koch Tables of Houses, northern latitudes are shown in a centre page column, covering from zero to 60 degrees of latitude.

To show this in action, turn further ahead to our John Jones Birth Calculation Sheet (page 174) and you'll see our final sum was 18 hours 32 minutes 34 seconds. We find the nearest round figure to that sum on the top of the page in our Tables of Houses, which is 18 hours 34 minutes 50 seconds.

We run our finger down the N. Lat. column and take the nearest round figure of latitude to Sydney (where John Jones was born) which is 34 degrees of latitude.

There are other valuable reference books especially prepared for Southern Hemisphere births and more detailed methods of calculation which most professional astrologers use. But, as beginners often tangle the two techniques with disastrous results, we have chosen to stay with the one that is easiest and yet still gives accurate figures.

COMPUTATION

Tools you need for chart calculation
All top professional astrologers have extensive libraries of reference works. You won't want to go to this expense at the outset of your studies, but there are certain essential 'tools' which no serious student can do without. These are as follows.

Blank Birth Chart forms. You can trace these off our sample forms or buy them from astrology bookshops.

Birth Calculation Sheets. You can copy these from our sample sheets.

Atlas or gazetteer. This is necessary for finding longitude and latitude of birthplaces anywhere in the world.

Ephemeris for all years of birth you wish to calculate. There are several different varieties of these, obtainable from astrology bookshops.

Tables of Houses. Again there are several varieties obtainable from astrology bookshops.

Special note on reference books

Minor differences do exist in data printed in various works of reference, such as atlases or gazeteers, tables of houses, etc. I use *Philip's New World Atlas* for longitude and latitude, *Koch Tables of Houses for Northern Latitudes*, and *Simplified Scientific Ephemeris* published by the Rosicrucian Fellowship. This last is supplied in separate volumes for each decade.

If you are checking our sample charts from reference works other than the above, you may find the data you read therein differs slightly from the data upon which I have based sample chart calculations.

Now, we'll list the steps in chart calculation, then set out a complete example.

Start-to-finish calculation planner

1. Obtain time, date and place of birth.
2. Ascertain longitude and latitude of birthplace.
3. Ascertain zone or standard time of birthplace.
4. Check if daylight saving time applied at time of birth.
5. Calculate GMT for time of birth.
6. Check if GMT altered date of birth.
7. Obtain S.T. for date of birth from ephemeris.
8. Calculate acceleration on interval.
9. Correct for longitude of birthplace.
10. Calculate local sidereal time at birth.
11. For Southern Hemisphere births only: *add* 12 hours to local sidereal time at birth.
12. Ascertain Ascendant, midheaven and house cusps from Tables of Houses for Northern Latitudes. For Southern Hemisphere births only, reverse signs on house cusps.

Never omit or forget any one of these steps, or your final calculation will be wrong.

Next, we'll put the planner into action with two cases of real individuals (whose names have been changed), one born in Australia (Southern Hemisphere) and one born in Bulgaria (Northern Hemisphere). You'll see how easy it is to follow the steps on the following Birth Calculation Sheets. It's well worth keeping a set of these sheets on hand whenever you're working on charts. They ensure you don't miss any step and if kept in a permanent file provide a quick-glance record of your completed work and overall progress.

With our two sample cases, we've chosen charts which demonstrate two of the problems which often trip up beginners.

In the first chart, the calculations require the application of the '24-hour rule'. As there are 24 hours of time in any day, always *subtract* 24 when the hours column exceeds 24 or add 24 when necessary (see line F). (See our John Jones sample Birth Calculation Sheet, line K.) Further, when (as shown at Line F on same sample sheet) the sidereal time at Greenwich (S.T.) is a lesser figure in hours than the time of birth to be subtracted therefrom, always add 24 hours to the S.T. hours column.

In the second chart, we show the effect of *sign interception*. When you begin erecting charts regularly, you'll observe that the Tables of Houses sometimes show the same sign on more than one house cusp, thus displacing other signs. These displaced (intercepted) signs are not left out. Each must be written in their correct counter-clockwise sequence but wholly within the appropriate house. (See Jean Smith sample chart.)

Remember, too, the natural order of the signs never varies. Aries is always followed by Taurus, next Gemini, next Cancer, next Leo, next Virgo, next Libra, next Scorpio, next Sagittarius, next Capricorn, next Aquarius, next Pisces.

The calculation method set out here is that suggested by Margaret Hone and other leading textbook authors. Other methods do exist but in my view this is by far the easiest for beginners, offers a high level of accuracy and is close to being 'mistake-proof'!

Case No. 1 (a Southern Hemisphere birth)
Birth details: John Jones, born at 11.40 a.m., 4 July 1961 at Sydney, N.S.W., Australia.

Blank

For noon ephemeris only

Birth Calculation Sheet

Name:

Birth details	Day	Month	Year
Birthdate of subject			
Birthplace of subject:			
Latitude of subject's birthplace:			
Longitude of subject's birthplace:			

	Hours	Minutes	Seconds
A. Birthtime of subject as stated:			
B. Zone or standard time of birthplace: (Subtract for eastern longitude; add for western)			
C. Daylight saving or summer time when applicable:			
D. GMT			
E. GMT date:			

	Hours	Minutes	Seconds
F. Sidereal time at Greenwich (noon GMT):			
G. Interval *to* or *from* noon: (Subtract when GMT = a.m. time; add when GMT = p.m. time)			
H. Acceleration in interval: (Rate = 10 seconds for every hour. Subtract or add as for line G above)			
I. Sidereal time at Greenwich at birth:			
J. Longitude equivalent of birthplace stated in time: (Subtract for western longitudes; add for eastern)			
K. Local sidereal time at birth:			
L. (Southern Hemisphere births only) Add 12 hours:			

M. House cusps as given in Northern Latitudes House Tables:
10th   11th   12th   1st   2nd   3rd

Reversed House cusps (Southern Hemisphere births only):
10th   11th   12th   1st   2nd   3rd

For noon ephemeris only

Birth Calculation Sheet

Name: John Jones

Birth details
Birthdate of subject
Birthplace of subject: Sydney
Latitude of subject's birthplace:
Longitude of subject's birthplace:

Day	Month	Year
4	7	61

33 : 51 South
151 : 18 East

	Hours	Minutes	Seconds
A. Birthtime of subject as stated:	11	40	00 a.m.
B. Zone or standard time of birthplace: (Subtract for eastern longitude; add for western)	−10	00	00
C. Daylight saving or summer time when applicable:	NIL		
D. GMT	1	40	00 a.m.

E. GMT date: **4.7.61**

	Hours	Minutes	Seconds
F. Sidereal time at Greenwich (noon GMT):	6	49	02
G. Interval *to* or *from* noon: (Subtract when GMT = a.m. time; add when GMT = p.m. time)	−10	20	00 a.m.
H. Acceleration in interval: (Rate = 10 seconds for every hour. Subtract or add as for line G above)	−00	01	40
I. Sidereal time at Greenwich at birth:	−20	27	22
J. Longitude equivalent of birthplace stated in time: (Subtract for western longitudes; add for eastern)	10	05	12
K. Local sidereal time at birth:	30	32	34
	−24	00	00
	6	32	34
L. (Southern Hemisphere births only) Add 12 hours:	12	00	00
	18	32	34

M. House cusps as given in Northern Latitudes House Tables:
　　10th 8♉　　11th 4♒　　12th 6♓　　1st 13♈　　2nd 18♉　　3rd 15♓

　　Reversed House cusps (Southern Hemisphere births only):
　　10th 8♋　　11th 4♌　　12th 6♍　　1st 13♎　　2nd 18♏　　3rd 15♐

Now, let's check the completed sheet through to ensure you understand the whys and wherefores of each step.

Lines A-E
John Jones was born at 11.40 a.m. in Sydney but Sydney's zone or standard time is 10 hours *ahead* and *east* of Greenwich. Hence we *subtract* 10 hours from 11.40 a.m. and find the GMT for John's birthtime is 1.40 a.m. having first checked that no daylight saving applied in Sydney when he was born.

Since a 1.40 a.m. GMT does not pass the preceding midnight, the GMT date of John's birth is the same as his actual date.

Line F
Sidereal time at Greenwich is found by looking in the ephemeris for 4 July 1961 under the column headed S.T. with the letters H.M.S. beneath, representing hours, minutes and seconds. (Some ephemeris show hours and minutes only.) Be sure you enter each figure in the appropriate column on your sheet. We must add 24 to the hours column here as 10 hours cannot be subtracted from 6 hours. This we have altered sidereal time (S.T.) from 6.49.02 to 30.49.02.

Lines G-H
The GMT of John's birth is 1.40 a.m. The interval between that time and the subsequent noon is 10 hours 20 seconds. The acceleration on that interval (at a rate of 10 seconds for every hour of time) = 100 seconds, expressed as 1 minute 40 seconds.

Again, always remember we are calculating with units of time, not decimals. Hence if your calculations require you to 'borrow' from minutes to seconds column, you 'borrow' 60 (seconds) and 'pay back' one minute. If you borrow from hours to minutes column, you borrow 60 (minutes) and pay back one (hour).

Lines I-K
The sum you now have on Line I is the sidereal time at Greenwich at John's birth. But because he was born in Sydney, we must now make the longitude calculation for this birthplace. Sydney's

longitude is 151 degrees 18 minutes *east*. We thus multiply the longitude by 4, which gives our answer in units of time as 604 minutes 72 seconds. There are 60 minutes in every hour and 60 seconds in every minute. This answer converts to 10 hours 5 minutes 12 seconds.

We *add* for eastern longitudes so we now add that figure, arriving at 30 hours 32 minutes 34 seconds. As there are only 24 hours per day, we must now subtract 24, so the figure becomes 6 hours 32 minutes 34 seconds.

Lines L-M

John *was* born in the Southern Hemisphere so we now *add* 12 hours. (This rule arises from the fact that any point in the Northern Hemisphere is separated from its opposite point in the Southern Hemisphere by 12 hours.)

Next we look up our final sum of 18 hours 32 minutes 34 seconds in the Tables of Houses *for the Northern hemisphere*. Take the closest figure to 18h 32m 34s (shown at head of tables page) which, you'll find, is 18h 34m 50s. Beneath this the tenth house cusp (or midheaven) is shown by letter M, followed by the degree and symbol of the sign occupying the midheaven. This is how it looks in the Tables book: M8♑ .

Now run your finger down the latitude column headed N. Lat. till you find the nearest round figure to Sydney's latitude of 33 degrees 51 minutes, which, you'll note, is 34 degrees.

Fill in the other house cusps now on your sheet. They are set out in the Tables book as:

XI (11th), XII (12th), A (Ascendant or 1st house cusp), II (2nd), III (3rd). From the Tables book they read as follows (taken to nearest round figure):

10th = 8♑ ; 11th = 4≈; 12th = 6♓ ; 1st = 13♈; 2nd = 18♉ ; 3rd = 15♊ .

Now, because John's birth was in the Southern Hemisphere we

reverse these house cusps to the opposite sign. (Check back to Chapter 4 if you haven't learnt by heart which sign is opposite to which, or the order of the signs themselves.)

The reversed house cusps now read:

10th = 8♋; 11th = 4♌; 12th = 6♍; 1st = 13♎; 2nd = 18♏; 3rd = 15♐.

This brings us at last to the point where we can begin the precise erection of John Jones' chart. Study the following diagram, check and recheck the steps if you don't thoroughly understand each one.

The house system we are using here is called the *Placidean House System*. Another house system, still widely used by some astrologers, is called the *Equal House System*, but that will not be discussed in this course.

The numbers printed round the centre of our diagram are of course the house numbers. As we saw in Chapter 3 the houses follow each other in a counter-clockwise direction. From the Houses Tables, we obtained the degree of each sign on each house cusp from tenth to third inclusive. How did we find the remaining fourth to ninth house cusps? Simple: by their opposing signs.

Remember, Aries always opposes Libra and vice versa; i.e., they appear exactly opposite to each other in the horoscope wheel. The other opposites are: Taurus and Scorpio; Gemini and Sagittarius; Cancer and Capricorn; Leo and Aquarius; and, Virgo and Pisces.

And you'll see from our diagram the opposing sign takes the same degree as its opposite. Our 8 degrees of Cancer on the tenth gives an 8 degrees of Capricorn on the fourth, and so on, round the wheel.

Case No. 2 (a Northern Hemisphere birth)
Birth details: Jean Smith, born at 8.10 p.m., 12 October 1950 at Ruse, Bulgaria.

For noon ephemeris only

Birth Calculation Sheet

Name: Jean Smith

Birth details

	Day	Month	Year
Birthdate of subject	12	10	50

Birthplace of subject: Ruse, Bulgaria
Latitude of subject's birthplace: 43 : 50 North
Longitude of subject's birthplace: 25 : 57 East

		Hours	Minutes	Seconds
A.	Birthtime of subject as stated:	8	10	00 p.m.
B.	Zone or standard time of birthplace: (Subtract for eastern longitude; add for western)	−2	00	00
C.	Daylight saving or summer time when applicable:		NIL	
D.	GMT	6	10	00 p.m.
E.	GMT date: **12.10.50**			

		Hours	Minutes	Seconds
F.	Sidereal time at Greenwich (noon GMT):	13	21	58
G.	Interval *to* or *from* noon: (Subtract when GMT = a.m. time; add when GMT = p.m. time)	+6	10	00 p.m.
H.	Acceleration in interval: (Rate = 10 seconds for every hour. Subtract or add as for line G above)	+0	01	00
I.	Sidereal time at Greenwich at birth:	19	32	58
J.	Longitude equivalent of birthplace stated in time: (Subtract for western longitudes; add for eastern)	+1	43	48
K.	Local sidereal time at birth:	21	16	46
L.	(Southern Hemisphere births only) Add 12 hours:	Not applicable		
		21	16	46

M. House cusps as given in Northern Latitudes House Tables:
    10th: 17≈ 11th: 0♈ 12th: 13♉ 1st: 14♓ 2nd: 8♋ 3rd: 28♋

    Reversed House cusps (Southern Hemisphere births only):
    10th   11th   12th   1st   2nd   3rd N/A

Now, again we'll check through the completed sheet to ensure no point has been left unexplained.

Lines A-E

Jean Smith was born at 8.10 p.m. in Ruse, Bulgaria, but Ruse's zone or standard time is 2 hours *ahead* and *east* of Greenwich. Hence we *subtract* 2 hours from 8.10 p.m., having first checked that no daylight saving applied in Ruse when she was born, and find GMT for Jean's birthtime is 6.10 p.m.

Since a 6.10 p.m. GMT does not pass the preceding midnight, the GMT date of Jean's birth is the same as her actual date.

Line F

As before, we found the sidereal time at Greenwich in the ephemeris, for 12 October 1950.

Lines G-H

The GMT of Jean's birth is 6.10 p.m. The interval between that time and the previous noon is 6 hours 10 minutes. The acceleration on that interval (at a rate of 10 seconds for every hour of time) = 60 seconds, expressed as 1 minute.

Lines I-K

The sum you now have on Line I is the sidereal time at Greenwich at Jean's birth. But because she was born at Ruse, we must now make the longitude calculation for this birthplace. Ruse's longitude is 25 degrees 57 minutes *east*. We thus multiply the longitude by 4 which gives our answer in units of time as 100 minutes 228 seconds. This answer converts to 1 hour 43 minutes 48 seconds.

We *add* for eastern longitudes so we now add that figure, arriving at 21 hours 16 minutes 46 seconds.

Lines L-M

Jean was born in the Northern Hemisphere so no addition of a further 12 hours is necessary and no reversal of the house cusps applies. We thus simply look up our final sum of 21 hours 16 minutes 46 seconds in the Tables of Houses for the Northern

Hemisphere. Take the closest figure to our final sum, which, you'll find is 21h 17m 49s, giving the midheaven (10th house cusp) as 17≈.

Now run your finger down the latitude column and you'll find the nearest round figure to Ruse's latitude of 43 degrees 50 minutes is 44 degrees.

Fill in the house cusps on your sheet taken to nearest round figure:

11th = 0♈; 12th = 13♉; 1st = 14♓; 2nd = 8♋; 3rd = 28♋.

That's all. So now we can also begin the precise erection of both John Jones' and Jean Smith's charts.

Study the sample charts, noting especially the interception of the signs of Virgo (intercepted in Jean's fourth house) and Pisces (intercepted in her tenth house).

Intercepted signs are always written in this manner.

CALCULATING PLANETARY POSITIONS

Our next move is to calculate the planet's exact positions for the time of birth of our two sample cases.

We'll take John Jones' chart first. Look in a noon ephemeris for the degrees and minutes of the Sun, Moon, Mercury, Venus and Mars on 4 July 1961. You don't need to adjust the positions of the other planets as they move so slowly each day, the change is minimal or non-existent.

You'll note the symbols of the planets at the top of the column. Always check, of course, by running your eye down the column to the required date that the planet you're dealing with did not change signs between the first day of the birth month and the date you're working on.

The change to the next sign if the planet is going direct (i.e., moving ahead) or to the previous sign if the planet is retrograding (i.e., backtracking) will be shown on the date it occurred in the column. The letter R beside a planet's degrees and minutes means it is retrograde. The letter D shows when the planet resumed direct motion.

On 4.7.61 the Sun   = 12.15 Cancer
        the Moon =   3.57 Aries
        Mercury   =   2.06 Cancer retrograde
        Venus   = 27.11 Taurus
        Mars   =   3.16 Virgo

But we remember that the GMT for John's birth was 1.40 a.m.
on 4.7.61, which is 10 hours 20 minutes *before* noon that day. So
to prepare to adjust the planet's positions we also list them for
3.7.61.

On 3.7.61 the Sun   = 11.18 Cancer
        the Moon = 19.54 Pisces
        Mercury   =   2.28 Cancer retrograde
        Venus   = 26.09 Taurus
        Mars   =   2.41 Virgo

Therefore we subtract the planetary positions on 4.7.61 from those
on 3.7.61. The following is the way we set them out in diagram form.

1. ☉ 12.15 ♋   2. ☽ 19.54 ♓   3. ☿ 2.06 ♋
     11.18   3.57 ♈   2.28 **R**
   ─────────   ──────────   ─────────
   00.57 ☉ Result   14.03 ☽ Result   0.22 ☿ Result

4. ♀ 27.11 ♉   5. ♂ 3.16 ♍
     26.09   2.41
   ─────────   ─────────
   1.02 ♀ Result   00.35 ♂ Result

You should be able to see how these figures were arrived at from
one glance in the cases of Sun, Venus and Mars.

In the case of the Moon, due to the planet changing signs from
Pisces to Aries during the two days we are working with, you must
remember that each sign contains 30 degrees, so the calculation
has to be made differently. In this situation, we subtract 19.54
degrees from 30 degrees to reach the figure of 10 degrees 6 minutes.
We then add 10 degrees 6 minutes to 3 degrees 57 minutes to give
a result of 14 degrees 3 minutes.

In the case of Mercury, due to the planet's retrograde motion on the dates in question, we must of course subtract the lower figure i.e., 2.06 from the higher 2.28.

The figures we have now for the final sum in each case represents the *daily motion* of each planet on the dates in question.

So, we now are ready for our next step which is to find the planets' positions (or longitudes) at the time of the birth. For these we need to use the Tables of Proportional Logarithms which are printed in the back of your ephemeris, to find the *log of the interval*.

These terms sound daunting to the unmathematical types, but in practice this step is very easy.

Remember, John's Sydney birthtime of 11.40 a.m. worked out at 1.40 a.m. GMT. So in our log tables we find the log for 10 hours 20 minutes (the interval of time between 1.40 a.m. and noon, remember?) which is 0.3660. This is the *log of the interval* we use for all our planetary adjustments.

We noted that the Sun's daily motion was 57 minutes. So we check in the log tables under 57 minutes and find that the log for this is 1.4025. Then we add the two logs together:

$$\begin{array}{r} 1.4025 \\ 0.3660 \\ \hline 1.7685 \end{array}$$

In our Table of Logs we find the nearest figure to 1.7685 is 1.7604. This figure (the anti-log) corresponds in the Minutes column of the Log Tables to 25 minutes. Hence we now know that between 1.40 a.m. (GMT of John's birth) and noon, the Sun travelled 25 minutes in what is termed 'celestial longitude'.

As John's GMT was 1.40 a.m. we must subtract 25 minutes from the position of the Sun on 4.7.61 to find the Sun's longitude at John's birth.

The above calculations are laid out below.

Sun's longitude at noon on 4.7.61	= 12.15 ♋
Sun's motion between 1.40 a.m. and noon	= 00.25
Sun's longitude at John's birth	= 11.50 ♋

We then go on to work out the positions of the Moon, Mercury, Venus and Mars in the same way, using the same *log of the interval*.

The results in diagram form are as follows:

Moon's longitude at noon on 4.7.61	= 3.57 ♈
Moon's motion between 1.40 a.m. and noon	= 6.03
Moon's longitude at John's birth	= 27.54 ♓

Because of the Moon's change from Pisces to Aries, this calculation requires one more comment. You must subtract first the 3 degrees 57 minutes from the Moon's position in Aries and then a further 2 degrees 6 minutes to make the complete subtraction of 6 degrees 3 minutes. When you subtract this 2 degrees 6 minutes from 30 degrees of Pisces, you find your answer is 27.54 of Pisces as set out above.

Next we look to Mercury. You remember this planet was retrograde so instead of subtracting our figure of 9 minutes, obtained by using our logs in the same manner as we did for the Sun, we *add* it to Mercury's position on the birthdate.

As a final check, the calculation for planets' positions are set out hereunder. Take the trouble to work them through yourself from your Log Tables as practice.

☉ 12.15 ♋	☽ 3.57 ♈	☿ 2.06 ♋ R	♀ 27.11 ♉	♂ 3.16 ♍
− 0.25	− 6.03	+ 0.09	− 0.27	− 0.15
11.50 ♋	27.54 ♓	2.15 ♋ R	26.44 ♉	3.01 ♍

Planetary calculation steps at a glance
Here's a quick checklist of steps you must use when calculating each planet's position.

1. Find position of planet at noon on birth-date.
2. Find position of planet at noon on day prior to birth or day after birth.
3. Complete addition *or* subtraction of above figures to find planet's daily motion.
4. Find log of interval between GMT and noon.
5. Find log of planet's motion.
6. Add logs (in decimals not units of time).

7. Find nearest figure in Log Tables.
8. Find anti-log of nearest figure in Log Tables.
9. Write in planet's position at noon.
10. Add *or* subtract from planet's position at noon (using units of longitude not decimals).
11. Result = longitude of planet's position at birth.

Now, we'll run through John's personal planets—Sun to Mars—using this list. Check your ephemeris to ensure you have thoroughly understood each step.

⊙ Sun—Calculation for birth position	Comment
1. 12.15♋ (Sun's noon position on 4.7.61) 2. 11.18♋ (Sun's noon position on 3.7.61) 3. 00.57 (Sun's daily motion)	Are you using correct days? Are you adding or subtracting?
4. 0.3660 (log of interval) 5. 1.4025 (log of sun's motion) 6. 1.7685 (log addition) 7. 1.7604 (nearest log)	Are you using decimals? Do it manually or by calculator.
8. 25′ (nearest anti-log)	
9. 12.15♋ (Sun's noon position) 10. −0.25 (+ or − from above) 11. 11.50♋ (Sun's birth position)	Have you checked they are the right days you're using? Are you adding or subtracting?

☽ Moon—Calculation for birth position	Comment
1. 3.57♈ (Moon's noon position on 4.7.61) 2. 19.54♓ (Moon's noon position on 3.7.61) 3. 14.03 (Moon's daily motion)	Have you remembered what to do if Moon changes signs?
4. 0.3360 (Log of interval) 5. 0.2325 (Log of Moon's motion) 6. 0.5985 (Log addition) 7. 0.5985 (Nearest log)	Decimal calculation here again.
8. 6.03 (Nearest anti-log)	
9. 3.57♈ (Moon's noon position) 10. −6.03 (+ or − from above) 11. 27.54♓ (Moon's birth position)	Have you remembered to use units of longitude here? Borrowing 60′ and paying back 1° when necessary
☿ Mercury—Calculation for birth position	Comment
1. 2.28♋ **R** (Mercury's noon position 4.7.61) 2. 2.06♋ (Mercury's noon position 3.7.61) 3. 0.22 (Mercury's daily motion)	Have you remembered what to do if a planet is retrograde?
4. 0.3660 (Log of interval) 5. 1.8159 (Log of Mercury's motion) 6. 2.1819 (Log addition) 7. 2.2041 (Nearest log)	Decimal calculation here again.
8. 9′ (Nearest anti-log)	
9. 2.06♋ **R** (Mercury's noon position) 10. +0.09 (+ or − from above) 11. 2.15♋ **R** (Mercury's birth position)	Have you checked that degrees and minutes are in correct column?

♀ Venus—Calculation for birth position	Comment
1. 27.11 ♉ (Venus' noon position on 4.7.61) 2. 26.09 ♉ (Venus' noon position on 3.7.61) 3. 1.02 (Venus' daily motion)	Have you remembered Venus' daily motion is fairly slow?
4. 0.3660 (Log of interval) 5. 1.3660 (Log of Venus' motion) 6. 1.7320 (Log addition) 7. 1.7270 (Nearest log)	Check again—you're using decimals here.
8. 27′ (Nearest anti-log)	
9. 27.11 ♉ (Venus' noon position) 10. – 27′ (+ or – from above) 11. 26.44 ♉ (Venus' birth position)	Back to units of longitude here. Borrow 60′ and pay back 1° when necessary?
♂ Mars—Calculation for birth position	Comment
1. 3.16 ♍ (Mars' noon position on 4.7.61) 2. 2.41 ♍ (Mars' noon position on 3.7.61) 3. 0.35 (Mars' daily motion)	Have you noted Mars' daily motion is slower than Venus?
4. 0.3660 (Log of interval) 5. 1.6143 (Log of Mars' motion) 6. 1.9803 (Log addition) 7. 1.9823 (Nearest log)	Decimal calculation here again.
8. 15′ (Nearest anti-log	
9. 3.16 ♍ (Mars' noon position) 10. – 15 (+ or – from above) 11. 3.01 ♍ (Mars' birth position)	Check again—are you placing minutes in correct column?

Now, we'll run through our second case, Jean Smith's personal planets—Sun to Mars—using our 'Planetary Calculation Steps at a Glance' list on pages 183-4. Jean, you'll recall was born at 8.10 p.m. on 12.10.50 in Ruse, Bulgaria.

⊙ Sun—Calculation for birth position	Comment
1. 19.34♎ (Sun's noon position on 13.10.50) 2. <u>18.35♎</u> (Sun's noon position on 12.10.50) 3. 0.59 (Sun's daily motion)	Are you using correct days? Are you adding or subtracting?
4. 0.5902 (Log of interval) 5. <u>1.3875</u> (Log of Sun's motion) 6. 1.9777 (Log addition) 7. 1.9823 (Nearest log)	Are you using decimals? Do it manually or by calculator.
8. 15′ (Nearest anti-log)	
9. 18.35♎ (Sun's noon position) 10. + <u>15′</u> (+ or − from above) 11. 18.50♎ (Sun's birth position)	Have you checked they are the right days you are using? Are you adding or subtracting?
☽ Moon—Calculation for birth position	Comment
1. 16.29♏ (Moon's noon position on 13.10.50) 2. <u>1.33♏</u> (Moon's noon position on 12.10.50) 3. 14.56 (Moon's daily motion)	Have you remembered what to do if the Moon changes signs?
4. 0.5902 (Log of interval) 5. <u>0.2061</u> (Log of Moon's motion) 6. 0.7963 (Log addition) 7. 0.7966 (Nearest log)	Decimal calculation here again!
8. 3.50′ (Nearest anti-log)	
9. 1.33♏ (Moon's noon position) 10. +3.50 (+ or − from above) 11. 5.23♏ (Moon's birth position)	Have you remembered to use units of longitude here? Borrowing 60′ and paying back 1° when necessary?

☿ Mercury—Calculation for birth position	Comment
1. 6.17♎︎ (Mercury's noon position 13.10.50) 2. 4.37♎︎ (Mercury's noon position 12.10.50) 3. 1.40 (Mercury's daily motion)	Have you remembered what to do if a planet is retrograde?
4. 0.5902 (Log of interval) 5. 1.1584 (Log of Mercury's motion) 6. 1.7486 (Log addition) 7. 1.7434 (Nearest log)	Decimal calculation here again.
8. 26′ (Nearest anti-log)	
9. 4.37♎︎ (Mercury's noon position) 10. + 26′ (+ or − from above) 11. 5.03♎︎ (Mercury's birth position)	Have you checked that degrees and minutes are in correct column?
♀ Venus—Calculation for birth position	Comment
1. 11.34♎︎ (Venus' noon position on 13.10.50) 2. 10.18♎︎ (Venus' noon position on 12.10.50) 3. 1.16 (Venus' daily motion)	Have you remembered Venus' daily motion is fairly slow?
4. 0.5902 (Log of interval) 5. 1.2775 (Log of Venus' motion) 6. 1.8677 (Log addition) 7. 1.8573 (Nearest log)	Check again you're using decimals here.
8. 20′ (Nearest anti-log)	
9. 10.18♎︎ (Venus' noon position) 10. +0.20 (+ or − from above) 11. 10.38♎︎ (Venus' birth position)	Back to units of longitude here. Borrow 60′ pay back 1° when necessary.

♂ Mars—Calculation for birth position	Comment
1. 12.31 ♐ (Mars' noon position on 13.10.50) 2. 11.47 ♐ (Mars' noon position on 12.10.50) 3. 0.44 (Mars' daily motion)	Have you noted Mars' daily motion is slower than Venus?
4. 0.5902 (Log of interval) 5. 1.5149 (Log of Mars' motion) 6. 2.1051 (Log addition) 7. 2.1170 (Nearest log)	Decimal calculation here again.
8. 11′ (Nearest anti-log)	
9. 11.47 ♐ (Mars' noon position) 10. +0.11 (+ or − from above) 11. 11.58 ♐ (Mars' birth position)	Check again—are you placing minutes in correct column?

Spot-check on planetary calculations

1. Ensure you are using the right two days for planet's positions, i.e., birth day and either *day before* or *day after* the birth. (If uncertain, re-read appropriate section.)
2. Ensure you are adding to or subtracting from the right day when calculating planet's daily motion.
3. Ensure you know whether each planet is going direct or retrograde. (This is shown in the ephemeris.)
4. Remember extra steps in calculation when planet changes signs between the two days under consideration. (Occurs most often in case of the Moon.)
5. Remember a.m. times require subtraction of interval between the stated time and subsequent noon. A time of 1.30 a.m. does not mean you subtract 1½ hours. You subtract 10½ hours.
6. Remember the only planet which travels fast enough to make a major difference between day of birth and day before or after birth is the Moon.
7. Ensure you haven't confused minutes with degrees or hours, or written in the wrong column. For example, the Moon can move more than 13 degrees between two days while the Sun moves as little as 57 minutes.
8. Remember longitude in planetary calculation is measured in

degrees, minutes and seconds. Time is measured in *hours, minutes and seconds.* With both longitude and time, you borrow in units of 60 minutes and pay back in units of one degree or one hour when calculating.

9. Always be sure you have the correct zone or standard time for place of birth. S.T. Meridian is the term used in reference works. Some countries have changed the S.T. Meridian in recent times. For example, New Zealand changed from S.T. Meridian 172 degrees 30 minutes east to 180 degrees 00 minutes east on 1 January 1946.

10. Never take a punt on whether or not daylight saving applied at hour and date of birth. Check it each time, remembering in certain periods in certain countries, clocks were advanced two hours instead of one. Whereas, again in New Zealand, for instance, in daylight saving periods from 1928 to 1946, clocks were advanced only 30 minutes.

N.B.—As mentioned earlier in this section, *Time Changes in the World,* by D. C. Doane, is the best reference work for checking both points 9 and 10 above.

Diagram showing hours of each day on horoscope chart

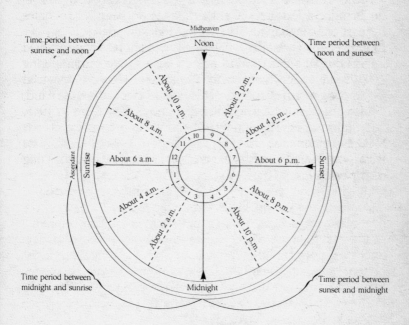

Divisions of Time

Placing planets on the chart

Turn now to the sample charts of our two cases—John and Jean—and note how and where the planets are placed following our calculations. (See pages 158-9.)

To make certain you understand every step in calculation, re-do those required for John Jones and Jean Smith yourself, using one of our blank Birth Calculation Sheets.

For further practice (especially if you haven't yet bought your 'tools of the trade', set out earlier), try your hand at calculating birth charts for individuals born on the same dates as our two examples, but at different times. This will impress upon you the importance of correct birthtime and correct calculation.

To illustrate visually: check the Divisions of Time diagram (page 192), noting which quadrants of the horoscope chart refer to which hours of day or night. This will be a handy mistake-eradicator in your future work. The Sun must be in the appropriate quadrant for the birthtime.

Thus, if you've calculated for an a.m. birth and the Sun appears in the bottom right-hand quadrant (which covers the sunset to midnight period) you have made an error in your calculations.

Compare now our finished sample charts. John Jones was born near noon and hence the Sun is in the upper left-hand quadrant near the tenth house cusp (midheaven). On the other hand, Jean Smith was born in mid-evening hours and hence the sun is in the bottom right-hand quadrant, in the fifth house. With beginners, this type of mistake usually occurs when dealing with Southern Hemisphere births because the adjustments for GMT have been overlooked or misunderstood.

On our finished chart diagrams for John Jones and Jean Smith, you will see the ten planets positioned in their appropriate houses. In John's chart, you'll observe Mars, though in Virgo, and Neptune, though in Scorpio, surrounded by a half-circle but placed in the house preceding their signs. Why? To occupy a house, each planet must be equal to, or more than the degree shown on the cusp of such house. Mars was only in 3 degrees 1 minute of Virgo yet the appropriate house cusp shows 6 degrees of Virgo. The same is true of Neptune in John's chart; likewise the Moon and also Mars in Jean's chart.

To ensure all the chart information is in front of you when you begin your personality analysis, I also advise students to write in the following as shown.

Under the heading 'B.T.Q.': which category the sign of each planet falls into.

Binaries   (B) because there are only two categories, for positive and negative.
Triples   (T) because there are three categories, for cardinal, fixed and mutable.
Quadruples (Q) because there are four categories, for fire, air, earth and water.

Under the heading 'Natal': the positions of the planets as calculated. Under the heading 'Major Aspects': their relationships to each other according to orb.

Next, I always suggest that students draw in (using coloured pens) the aspects as calculated. Red for hard aspects; green for easy ones.

This is a very helpful habit to learn. It shows the chart's overall pattern at a glance, helps you pick out important configurations instantly and emphasizes stress on both quadrants and houses.

So, here we are at last! At the end of the heavy mathematical bit and ready to tackle in-depth personality analysis. To many students, the mathematics of astrology constitutes a discouraging stumbling-block. But, as we said in the beginning of this section, the calculations do not need mathematical genius—just care and patience in mastering them. And they must be correct or your analysis will be thrown miles off course.

Nevertheless, as American author Isabel Hickey remarked in her lengthy work *Astrology: A Cosmic Science*: 'If you are like this author you will be ready to throw up your hands when you are studying the mathematics involved. But don't quit. Like driving a car, it becomes an automatic process after it is learned. The ones who have the most difficulty with the mathematics are always the best interpreters of the chart.'

Personally, I feel her last sentence is a little too strongly stated. But, I do agree that the student or practitioner who approaches the science of astrology primarily as a mathematician can often lose sight of the clear-cut 'topography' of human personality that the horoscope chart offers in a morass of competing calculations and conflicting potentials.

Computer charts

If you wish to dodge the time and trouble required to calculate a chart yourself, it's worth mentioning that most major cities now have computer services for this express purpose. This is not markedly expensive as a rule.

The computer works in the usual manner—i.e., the birth data is fed in and the print-out emerges with the chart drawn and planetary positions calculated and in place, together with their aspects.

Many professional astrologers nowadays order computer charts to save time. I, myself, rarely use them and I consider it vital for students to understand the mechanics of chart erection, if only to double-check on the print-out. (Computers are sometimes as fallible as human beings!)

Solar charts

This term is one you may run across from time to time. It means the chart has been prepared without birthtime.

Solar charts, in my view, should only be used as general indicators of an individual's personality patterns because, without the birthtime, the house cusps cannot be calculated and the emphasis on the twelve life sectors cannot be examined. Added to this, precise calculations as to planetary aspects cannot be made either.

TEST EXERCISE

Now that you've put yourself through the hoops with John Jones' and Jean Smith's charts, both of which contain traps for the unwary, try yourself out with an easier chart calculation.

This time our subject is a lady we'll call Mary Brown, born at 9.15 p.m. on 24 June 1946, in Wickford, Essex, England.

Remember, as she was born in England you won't have to worry about zone standard time. However, in case you don't have *Time*

Changes in the World available, we note that one hour summertime applied at the time of her birth.

Prepare Mary Brown's chart in full, completing the Birth Calculation Sheet as well. When you've finished, check your result in the Model Answer section at the end of this chapter, where you'll find Mary Brown's completed chart plus completed Calculation Sheet and correct planetary positions.

If you've really learnt your stuff, you should be able to whip through Mary Brown's chart as easily as a knife through cream cheese!

MODEL ANSWER

Northern Hemisphere birth example

Cardinal signs 5
Fixed signs   3
Mutable signs   2
Positive signs   5
Negative signs 5

Name: Mary Brown

G. 8.15 p.m.
B. Wickford, England
S. Placidean

FIRE signs   2
AIR signs   3
EARTH signs 2
WATER signs 3

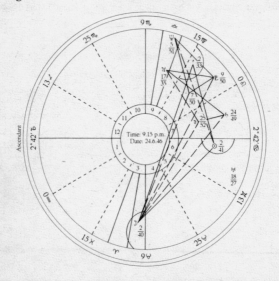

B.T.Q.	Planet	Natal	Major Aspects
P C A	9♆ Neptune	5.15♎	✳ ♇
P M A	6♅ Uranus	18.27♓	
N C W	7♄ Saturn	24.59♋	
P C A	9♃ Jupiter	17.35♎	✳ ♇ ☐ ♄
N M E	8♂ Mars	2.33♍	
N C W	7☉ Sun	2.41♋	✳ ☽ ✳ ☌ ☐ ♆
P F F	8♀ Venus	7.50♌	☌ ♇ ✳ ♆
N C W	7☿ Mercury	25.52♋	☐ ♃ ☌ ♄
N F E	3☽ Moon	2.40♑	☐ ♇ ☐ ☿ ☐ ♀ △ ☌ ☐ ♄
P F F	8♇ Pluto	9.50♌	

For noon ephemeris only

Birth Calculation Sheet

Name: Mary Brown

Birth details

	Day	Month	Year
Birthdate of subject	24	6	46

Birthplace of subject: Wickford, England

Latitude of subject's birthplace: 0 : 31 East

Longitude of subject's birthplace: 51 : 37 North

	Hours	Minutes	Seconds
A. Birthtime of subject as stated:	9	15	00 p.m.
B. Zone or standard time of birthplace: (Subtract for eastern longitude; add for western)	—	—	—
C. Daylight saving or summer time when applicable:	1	00	00
D. GMT	8	15	00 p.m.
E. GMT date: **24.6.46**			

	Hours	Minutes	Seconds
F. Sidereal time at Greenwich (noon GMT):	6	08	08
G. Interval *to* or *from* noon: (Subtract when GMT = a.m. time; add when GMT = p.m. time)	+8	15	00 p.m.
H. Acceleration on interval: (Rate = 10 seconds for every hour. Subtract or add as for line G above)	0	01	23
I. Sidereal time at Greenwich at birth:	14	24	31
J. Longitude equivalent of birthplace stated in time: (Subtract for western longitudes; add for eastern)	+	02	04
K. Local sidereal time at birth:	14	26	35
L. (Southern Hemisphere births only) Add 12 hours:	Not applicable		
	14	26	35

M. House cusps as given in Northern Latitudes House Tables:
   10th 9♏   11th 25♏   12th 13♐   1st 2.42♑   2nd 0♒   3rd 15♓

   Reversed House cusps (Southern Hemisphere births only): N/A
   10th   11th   12th   1st   2nd   3rd

Calculation of planetary positions for Mary Brown's chart

Logarithm of interval: 0.4638

House positions:

10th	9 ♏		1st	2.42 ♑
11th	25 ♏		2nd	0.0 ♒
12th	13 ♐		3rd	15 ♓

☉ 3.18 ♋	☽ 27.42 ♈	☿ 26.49 ♋
2.21	12.08 ♉	25.22
0.57 ☉ Result	14.26 ☽ Result	1.27 ♀ Result
2.41 ♋	2.40 ♉	25.52 ♋

♀ 8.37 ♌	♂ 2.55 ♍
7.26	2.21
1.11 ♀ Result	0.34 ♂ Result
7.50 ♌	2.33 ♍

Note

When you're satisfied that your accuracy in calculation is unerring, the above method of recording planetary positions in reference files is quick and handy for future checking.

If you still find difficulty in deciding how we arrived at the above result in the case of each planet, go back and work through the step-by-step examples we gave earlier in this chapter.

Remember, too, that Mary Brown's chart is another example of the Moon changing her sign in the two days we have calculated with, i.e., the actual day of Mary's birth and the day following as she was born at an hour later than noon.

Don't forget, either, that we obtain our final result—the planet's precise position at time of birth—by using logarithms and anti-logarithms as described earlier in this chapter. Most ephemeris contain tables of logs set out in easy-to-follow form.

6.

INTEGRATING ASCENDANT, SUN AND MOON

Now, at long last, the end really *is* in sight! We've painstakingly collected every piece in the jigsaw puzzle of human personality, looked it over and decided how and where it is going to fit — every piece that is, except the final three vital pieces: the Ascendant-Sun-Moon blend, otherwise known as 'the Big Three'. And a very significant trio they are. Because between them, they reveal the total impact each personality has on the world around it, and the immediate impression made upon others.

Their distinctive blend, like a personal signature, explains why some people appear easy to understand and quite predictable in behaviour, or the absolute opposite. Both these effects result from the Big Three occupying compatible signs and elements in the first instance, incompatible signs and elements in the second.

Incidentally, here too is where we find the immediate answer to the oft-repeated complaint, heard mostly from laymen: "I've got two Leo friends and they're as different as chalk and cheese!" The said two friends are not "as different as chalk and cheese" at all. Their Ascendants merely create a different initial impression, either boosting or baulking Leo traits.

To illustrate: A Leo individual with an Aries Ascendant is obviously going to come on strong with the forceful, extroverted fire energies stoking each other. A Leo individual with a Capricorn Ascendant won't — because cautious, matter-of-fact earth energies tend to throw rocks on the Leo fire.

Nevertheless, both Leos will demonstrate typical Lion personality traits when the chips are finally down. Why? Because, to use an analogy, the Ascendant is really only the icing on the cake, the

Sun sign is the cake itself and the Moon sign indicates the ingredients used to make the cake. Or, to put it all into more technical terms: the Big Three allow us to examine human personality at three levels.

The Ascendant (also called the Rising sign because it actually *was* rising in the heavens at the time of birth) represents the *projected personality*—the mask we put on when we leap out of bed each morning to face the world. In a sense, the Ascendant is a kind of camouflage, implying the way we want others to regard us—a cloak we don to hide the true self and the secret inner needs.

Ascending sign behaviour shows up most vividly in first contact with other people, when we are putting our best foot (and face) forward to make what *we* consider to be the most favourable impression. If our contacts with certain individuals or groups remain in the casual acquaintance category, both parties will probably never see more than each others' Ascendant behaviour. The surface cover will never be broken through until and if opportunities arise for closer contact or intimacy—often with illusion-shattering effects.

However, some textbook authors regard the Ascendant as so enormously significant, they tab a subject with it. e.g. James is a Piscean with a Virgo Sun. Jane is a Leo with a Scorpio Sun. Personally, I do not ascribe quite that much importance to the Ascendant but I never underestimate it either. Always remember the sign and degree of the Ascendant dictate the signs and degrees of the other eleven houses of the horoscope, thus spreading its influence into other life sectors and acting as a kind of *overlay* to the entire chart.

The Sun sign represents the *ego* drive, the core of our being, the true, unalterable self. No matter how forcefully other factors in the chart disguise, divert or thwart the thrust of the Sun's energy, it will always find a way around them, obviously or surreptitiously directing the individual's life.

Writer Gertrude Stein, who was famous for her apt statements in the earlier decades of this century, once said: 'A rose is a rose is a rose.' The same words can be applied to Sun Signs: 'A Virgo is a Virgo is a Virgo.' Nothing, but nothing, changes the *sense of the self* symbolized by the Sun sign. Astrologers who ignore that only do so at their peril. So always remember this in identifying basic ego drives in astro-analysis.

On the other hand, never overdo the emphasis on the Sun sign. The popular press has done horrifying disservice to the great science of astrology for years by hammering away on the Sun sign theme: by printing so-called 'daily forecasts' linked only to Sun signs and hence generalized to the point of becoming meaningless; by churning out concoctions of waffle, usually entitled something like 'Choose Your Ideal Lover by the Stars', again relying only on Sun signs.

The totally personal science of astrology can never be mass-marketed in this crass manner. And, sadly, these publications hand ammunition to the knockers, sceptics and bigots against whose uninformed attacks serious astrological analysis has always had to battle.

The last member of the Big Three group is *the Moon sign*. This represents *the secret self,* the instinctive responses, the imprinted emotional and habit patterns of each personality. For much of daily living, these are kept firmly under wraps but that does not mean they are insignificant in affecting the way each personality operates.

Moon sign behaviour is most visible in times of crisis or trauma, and when an individual is under the influence of alcohol or drugs. Any one of these situations is capable of knocking out the upper two levels of personality to reveal the secret self, hiding away beneath them. The Ancient Romans had a saying—*In vino veritas* (literally, 'When drunk, the truth'). A neat way of noting that when the acquired modes of civilized, socially conditioned behaviour are peeled away, there is no more kidding around. The hidden parts, pleasant or unpleasant, are revealed in all their glory!

To illustrate: A male scientist with whom I had an instructive but generally unrewarding association for several years was a Libran with a Scorpio Ascendant and the Moon in Aquarius. When stone cold sober, his Scorpio Ascendant kept him wary and intuitively tuned in to the motivations of others. His Libran Sun ensured he wouldn't make waves, push himself obtrusively or behave undiplomatically.

But when, as my ancient great-aunt used to remark he 'bent his elbow' (a Victorian euphemism for heavy drinking), the change was startling, mind-boggling.

Alcohol, having made short work of the restraining Ascendant and Sun, let the Aquarian Moon loose with a vengeance, and with all the intellectual arrogance, superiority and condenscension inherent in the negative traits of the sign. He would survey all before him, as from Olympian heights, and announce: 'I'm the most intelligent man I've ever met. In fact, I think I'm the most intelligent man in the world.'

Being a Virgo myself, my usual reply to that was: 'Wow! And to think in all these years I never realized it!'

To understand whether the Big Three will work together, harmoniously or inharmoniously, we must now re-check visualization of the twelve signs discussed in Chapter 1. So if you think you may still be a trifle hazy or have forgotten sign symbolism, go back and read the chapter again now.

Indeed, visualization is such an invaluable key to astrological understanding that I first thought of entitling this chapter 'How to Live with your Animals'! Because that's just what coping with the Ascendant-Sun-Moon blend adds up to!

After all, eight of the twelve signs are depicted by real live animals: the Ram, the Bull, the Crab, the Lion, the Scorpion, the Centaur, the Goat and the Fish. Three are depicted by human figures: the Twins, the Virgin and the Water-Bearer. Biologically, Man is also an animal (descended from the apes if Darwin was right). Thus the only inanimate member of the twelve is the Scales.

So let's look now at a trio of zodiac animals in action. Let's say we're considering a subject who has an Aries Ascendant, Capricorn Sun and Cancer Moon. Think carefully of how a real ram, a real mountain goat and a real crab behave in their natural habitat. The dashing, curly-horned ram leading his flock with an eye for every ewe in his charge. The nimble, bearded billy-goat, leaping from crag to crag in his never-ending climbs, his little herd following obediently behind him. The hard-shelled, silent crab, peering warily and solitarily out from his rock under the sea.

All very different creatures, aren't they? Yet anyone with the above blend has got to handle this trio of pretty tough animals — one ram, one goat and one crab, all struggling for supremacy within the psyche, all pulling furiously in completely different directions as they strive to satisfy their vastly differing needs.

Hence, the inner tension generated by clashing Ascendant, Sun and Moon signs is so divisive that individuals with this type of blend often get the feeling they've been struck with a split personality. Not so, of course. But such blends do require judicious handling and a fair go given to the needs of each 'animal' at each level. (By the way, American psychologist/astrologer Noel Tyl and leading textbook author Grant Lewi both published excellent work on Sun-Moon blends in personality analysis. See recommended library list at the end of this course.)

Of course, dealing with clashes between the Big Three is easier said than done! But once you learn how to visualize vividly, and to appreciate that the Ascendant, Sun and Moon are rather like entities living in the human mind, you can almost hear them fighting it out as each tries to grab control of the personality and push it in the direction each wants to go.

Let's dramatize a typical clash scene with a humourous example and listen in to the mind of our Aries Ascendant, Capricorn Sun and Cancer Moon subject. We'll imagine he's a young male, spotting an attractive girl in a bar.

RAM ASCENDANT:
Man, look at that. Let's flash across right now and chat her up. She's exactly our type!

GOAT SUN:
Hold it, stupid. I'm not going to let you make a fool of us by accosting a perfect stranger in a public place. Anyway, I've got work to do. We're going to have an early night.

CRAB MOON:
Of course, neither of you two ego-maniacs would bother to think about *me*, would you? I'm not into one-night stands, thanks very much, Ram. And I'm not a workaholic like you, Goat. Haven't either of you heard of emotional rapport? No! You wouldn't even know how to spell it!

Once you've calculated your own Ascendant, Sun and Moon signs, try listening in to these 'conversations' going on in your own mind. Especially when you have to make an important move or decision that might suit the needs of one of the Big Three but upset the other two. That's when the 'arguments' within are loudest and that's when you often find yourself well and truly on the horns of a dilemma—torn in two or more directions at once.

Remember, you can't ignore any one of the Big Three or pretend its needs do not exist. If you try you'll only push it underground where the repressed demand can work up a whole heap of trouble, sometimes revealing itself in physical ailments—which point suggests now would be a good time to list the areas of the body which the twelve signs rule, i.e. emphasize.

1. Aries, the Ram .... Head and organs therein.
2. Taurus, the Bull .... Neck, throat and shoulders.
3. Gemini, the Twins .... Hands, arms, lungs and nervous system.
4. Cancer, the Crab .... Breasts, stomach and glandular system.
5. Leo, the Lion .... Heart, back and cardiac system.
6. Virgo, the Virgin .... Intestines and alimentary system.
7. Libra, the Scales .... Kidneys.
8. Scorpio, the Scorpion .... Sexual organs and reproductive system.
9. Sagittarius, the Centaur .... Hips, thighs and hepatic system.
10. Capricorn, the Goat .... Knees and skeletal system.
11. Aquarius, the Water-Bearer .... Calves, ankles and circulatory system.
12. Pisces, the Fish .... Feet and lymphatic system.

The above list spotlights the vulnerable bodily areas specified for each sign. Problems can arise at any stage during the lifetime in the bodily areas ruled by whatever signs occupy the Ascendant, Sun and Moon positions. The sign on the cusp of the sixth house in each chart will give further clues to potential health problems. 'Potential' is always the operative word.

Thus, this does not mean that when Aries, for instance, is powerfully placed you're certain to suffer from headaches or injuries to the head, or that Aquarius will always supply you with varicose veins and/or weak ankles.

Yet an individual who ruthlessly tries to repress the demands of an Aries Moon, for example, often *does* experience severe headaches. And many who try to wipe Aquarius out of their charts *do* suffer circulatory ailments some time in their lives.

So, the way to help prevent problems, in health or otherwise, is to understand your own Big Three. See what each wants and apportion your time accordingly and evenly.

To take an example from my own life. Here's how I try to live in reasonable harmony with my set of 'animals'—namely, a Sagittarian Ascendant, Virgo Sun and Moon dead on the cusp of Sagittarius and Capricorn.

Scene, on waking up to a bright summer morning.

CENTAUR ASCENDANT (Breezily):
Hey, people, what a day! Let's thunder down to the surf right now. Salt water's good for us horses. And we might run into a few stallions or mares from my herd. Kick a few ideas around with them!

VIRGIN SUN (Reprovingly):
Not yet! I was up till one in the morning, trying to catch up the worktime you wasted yesterday. Anyway, I've just discovered a fascinating theory I want to investigate. That will take me to lunchtime at least . . .

GOAT MOON (Interrupting grimly):
Surfing! Theories! What a double! A fact of life which has obviously eluded both of you is that it costs money to live. Money does *not* grow on trees or out of surfing or chasing theories. Our job is analysing charts. And *that's* what we're going to do right now!

I've deliberately described this little fracas in light vein, but when it's happening in everyday life such conflicts are not too funny. Still, I strive to solve mine by parcelling out my day (without fear or favour) between the three of them: the Centaur, who's got me into more than enough trouble; the Virgin who makes me work harder than I really want; and the Goat, who's always nagging on about money.

I live by the beach and surf at least once a day in good weather, which keeps the Centaur fairly happy. I do make time to follow up new research and write, which ensures the Virgin doesn't fuss too much. I do complete one or more charts per day so the Goat can show his face at the bank each week with a passable air of confidence.

You can do the same with your Big Three. Understand each one thoroughly. Identify and isolate their prime needs. Then try to satisfy these needs. The daily programme is, naturally, a lot easier to plan if the Big Three are compatible. But even if they are as basically 'anti' each other as my Centaur and Virgin (that sporty, casual, slapdash Centaur pulling like crazy against the prissy, proper, finicky Virgin), you and everyone else can make them work together better if you try.

Now, we'll look at the twelve *projected personalities* as shown by the twelve Ascendants. Again, these are set out in brief outline to allow you to form your own conclusions as well and must, in each case, be linked with the visualization of the sign's symbolic figure.

Remember, too, when any sign (Ascendant or other) occupies a cusp position (this is, on the borderline between two signs), some of the qualities of both will manifest.

PROJECTED PERSONALITY AS SHOWN BY THE ASCENDANT

Asc=Aries
An Aries Ascendant makes your projected personality that of an energetic, impulsive, enterprising individual, who is always willing to take a chance and likes to shine in social situations.

Aries also predisposes towards rashness, lack of consideration for others, careless haste, plus quick-tempered and brusque behaviour.

Asc=Taurus

A Taurus Ascendant makes your projected personality that of a patient, conservative and calm individual, who is generally easy-going, but nevertheless can always be relied upon to get on with the business of living.

Taurus also predisposes towards great acquisitiveness, too much emphasis on money and possessions, plus marked stubbornness.

Asc=Gemini

A Gemini Ascendant makes your projected personality that of a bright, versatile individual who enjoys plenty of social life and can talk anybody in or out of anything.

Gemini also predisposes towards extreme changeability of interests and attitudes, shallowness and lack of deep understanding.

Asc=Cancer

A Cancer Ascendant makes your projected personality that of a sympathetic, reserved and home-loving individual, who is notable for good taste and loyalty to family and friends.

Cancer also predisposes towards a tendency to harbour resentment over imagined slights, fussiness and over-protective attitudes.

Asc=Leo

A Leo Ascendant makes your projected personality that of a confident, pleasure-loving, dignified individual who likes to be in command and does everything in a big way.

Leo also predisposes towards bossiness, personal vanity and the desire to organize everyone and everything.

Asc=Virgo

A Virgo Ascendant makes your projected personality that of a quiet, conventional, reserved person who enjoys work but does not pursue what is generally regarded as 'a good time'.

Virgo also predisposes towards a rather aloof exterior manner, a tendency to be over-critical and very finicky about personal neatness and cleanliness.

Asc=Libra

A Libra Ascendant makes your projected personality that of a gracious, diplomatic, friendly individual, who enjoys good conversation and artistic, well-appointed surroundings.

Libra also predisposes towards superficiality, indecisiveness, vacillation and a tendency to lean on others rather than make up your own mind.

Asc=Scorpio

A Scorpio Ascendant makes your projected personality that of an intense, very determined individual who is prepared to overcome any odds in the pursuit of personal goals.

Scorpio also predisposes towards jealousy, suspiciousness, periods of brooding resentment and a very icy form of self-control.

Asc=Sagittarius

A Sagittarius Ascendant makes your projected personality that of an energetic, friendly, outgoing individual who is optimistic in outlook and frank in conversation.

Sagittarius also predisposes towards boasting, tall-story telling and fickleness in associations. You can accept neither constraint or restraint.

Asc=Capricorn

A Capricorn Ascendant makes your projected personality that of a practical, hard-working and ambitious individual, who enjoys serious conversations, and conventional entertainments.

Capricorn also predisposes towards lack of real spontaneity, a rather calculating approach to people, and a strong desire to organize.

Asc=Aquarius

An Aquarius Ascendant makes your projected personality that of an idealistic, rather dogmatic, sociable individual with exceptionally high standards, but unorthodox, even rebellious attitudes.

Aquarius also predisposes towards lack of tact, a somewhat patronizing attitude and sometimes eccentric behaviour which can be 'cranky' or coldly objective.

Asc = Pisces

A Pisces Ascendant makes your projected personality that of a gentle, sympathetic individual, who is always willing to lend a helping hand to anyone in trouble—whether they deserve it or not!

Pisces also predisposes towards passivity and inactivity plus an extreme lack of self-confidence which limit your chances and make you prone to odd periods of laziness.

To set the significance of the Ascendant firmly in your mind, here are some further angles upon it by leading astrological textbook authors.

Dr H. L. Cornell:
The Ascendant determines largely the physical appearance, description of the body, height, weight, the degree of vitality etc. and is very important to study in connection with health and disease.

Isabel Hickey:
Think of the Ascendant as a window through which you look at the world. Each window is of a different shape and colour, changing the way we see things.

Margaret Hone:
The Ascendant is of the greatest importance, because when delineating a chart, every trait of character deduced from any other part of the chart, must be considered in relation to the *type of person* evincing it, as shown by the Ascending sign.

Jeff Mayo:
The Ascendant corresponds to that aspect of man we call personality. Jung speaks of the Persona, from the Greek persona, meaning a mask, a pretended character, worn by an actor. Because the Ascendant derives from the horizon of a person's birthplace, and is determined by the Earth's rotation, an interesting yet nevertheless consistent fact becomes clear: the personality or persona is an adopted attitude largely conditioned and impressed upon an individual by his particular Earth-environment. It can be the face a man wears whilst he projects

himself into his business and social activities, concealing much of his true character that only his intimates — and often not even they — know exists.

All four of the foregoing quotes stress the need to give full consideration to the Ascendant in every chart you draw and analyse. The entire grab-bag of conflicting traits, attitudes and potentials of each individual have to be thrust through the channel of the Ascendant, rather like water being pumped through a conduit.

If the Ascendant blends comfortably with the Sun sign and Moon sign too, the flow is easy and steady. If the Ascendant conflicts, it can act like an obstruction in the conduit, diverting the flow.

This adds up to another excellent reason why you should always consider another person's chart in depth before you enter into any binding association with that person.

My mother, a good-looking Aquarian actress, always used to say: 'Those who haste to marriage repent it at their leisure.' (I might add she certainly *did* practise what she preached on that point, having insisted on my Libran father courting her for seven years before she walked up the aisle!) And Mother was right. It is only too easy, if you leap into a permanent relationship after only a brief acquaintance, to find you have bought the proverbial pig in a poke. Or to put it into astrological terms—you have teamed up with your partner's Ascendant, not his/her true self.

The Ascendant will do its job and keep the mask in place, the party manners in operation for a time but *not* forever. Then, when the gilt's off the gingerbread and the sweet talking done, you may find you are stuck with a stranger who is the true self of your partner. If, by some stroke of remarkable good fortune, you find you like the true self bit as much as the Ascendant bit, all's well. If not, then you're up to your ears in very troubled waters indeed!

Hence, it's always best to check out his/her chart (in business as well as love partnerships) and look before you leap. Better to be safe than sorry!

Finally, remember the Ascendant must never be guessed at, picked out of a printed textbook table, or sloppily calculated. Not only will the wrong Ascendant give an entirely misleading impression of the personality you're analysing, it will also throw out of place the other eleven house cusps, planetary positions, etc.

Always check the Sun's position (see diagram, page 191) in each completed chart. If the Sun is in the wrong hours quadrant, the Ascendant has been miscalculated.

As we saw in the preceding chapter, you must know and take into consideration both birthtime and birthplace as well as birthdate when calculating each Ascendant. There is no way of short-cutting.

There is however, one further check you can make as to the choice of the correct Ascendant — your subject's *physical appearance*. This is not a sure-fire guide because the Sun sign, Moon sign and planets rising in or around the first house also contribute to looks, height, weight, etc. But physical appearance checks *do* help.

Ascendant	*Characteristic appearance*
Aries	Ram-like: reddish hair, sometimes curly, pointed chin-line.
Taurus	Bull-like: heavier build, heavier jaw, large, bull-like eyes.
Gemini	Taller, slimmer build, alert expression, forward-leaning walk.
Cancer	Crab-like: broader face, heavy-lidded eyes, very small hands and feet.
Leo	Lion-like: thick mane of hair, eyes that can stare like a cat, padding walk.
Virgo	Virginal: oval face, smaller neater features, aloof expression.
Libra	Well put together: symmetrical features, rounded chin, air of refinement.
Scorpio	Intimidating: piercing eyes, arrow-heads brows, awkward walk.
Sagittarius	Horse-like: leaner, lankier body, large teeth, purposeful walk.
Capricorn	Goat-like: long, narrow face, thin neck, deep-set, serious eyes.
Aquarius	Strikingly attractive: square-cut face, wide-open eyes, brilliant smile.

Pisces   Fish-like: full mouth, dreamy eyes, narrow
                    shoulders.

So that's it. We've now got everything together and we're ready
to analyse a complete sample chart.

We know the signs from Chapter 1, the planets from Chapter
2, the houses from Chapter 3, the planetary aspects from Chapter
4, the calculation techniques from Chapter 5; and lastly, the
integration of Ascendant, Sun and Moon from this chapter.

It sounds a lot to keep in mind all at once, doesn't it? But the
more charts you do, the easier accurate chart synthesis becomes.
The Oxford Dictionary defines 'synthesis' as 'building up of
separate elements . . . of conceptions or propositions or facts, into
a connected whole'. And that's just what we're going to tackle next.

7.
ANALYSING THE COMPLETED CHART

'Oh, Heavens! There's so much to remember! Where do I start?'
This woeful cry is typical of all beginners in the field of astrological
analysis—including myself when I first tried to synthesize a chart
back in the 1960s.

There are, of course, almost as many ways of approaching
synthesis as there are rails on a railroad or stars in the sky. No
teacher should force his/her technique on a student. Each individual
must experiment by trial and error to find the method that's right
for their way of thinking, their concept of astrological science.

I shall however, in this chapter set down a step-by-step outline
of my style of synthesis. You'll find other step-by-step approaches
in Margaret Hone's work and Jeff Mayo's. (See library list at end
of this course.)

Before we begin, I must once more sound the warning bell. Don't
hurry a synthesis. I still spend at least four hours on each chart
I analyse. Don't jump to premature conclusions. Wise readers never
judge a book by its cover: good analysts never permit first
impressions of a chart to fool them. Don't let your client pressurize
you. This leads to the dangerous error of telling clients what they
want to hear and damages your impartiality of judgement.

It is also important to bear in mind whenever you analyse
another's chart, that your *own* personality patterns must affect your
style and approach. Oddly enough, I have noted that some lecturers
and textbook writers are positively coy about stating their own
Ascendant, Sun and Moon positions to students and readers. In
my view, clients are entitled to know this if they so desire because
the Big Three do affect the whole tenor of your analysis.

If you have the time, it's well worth your while taking a short course in basic psychology in addition to this or any other course in astro-analysis. Many technical colleges or evening class institutes offer these. Such training will teach you scientific method in personality analysis and prevent you from falling into the vagaries of the fortune-teller.

As Noel Tyl says in one book of his twelve-volume treatise on astrology and psychology, a knowledge of the behavioural sciences is invaluable to the astrologer. Tyl adds: 'The astrologer identifies with countless levels of psychology and experience; he himself grows in his service to others.' In our final chapter, we'll have more to discuss about precisely what makes a good or a bad analyst. But now, we'll start our step-by-step synthesis.

As I often tell my own clients, chart synthesis is rather like putting a probe down into the centre of the earth. Watching, recording each change in the strata along the way but pressing inexorably downward — deeper and deeper — to the centre of the psyche, the gut of being.

As we set off, your first glance at the surface terrain may give the impression that the whole scene is that of a green and pleasant land. Everything looking bright and well-cared-for, nothing prickly or dangerous showing anywhere. But as we go deeper, we may find that at the centre there is a molten turmoil of resentments, repressions, anger. Or, of course, vice versa. The surface may look a bit forbidding but beneath all is peace and serenity.

On the next page you'll find a blank Personality Profile form. Use this, if you wish, for your first attempts at synthesis. Later you'll probably want to design one to suit your own special style. Next again, we'll see a Personality Profile form completed for the actual individual we called John Jones and whose birth chart we calculated in an earlier chapter. These personality profiles are abridged versions of the complete analysis, designed to keep you on the track and to ensure you don't inadvertently miss any major step.

When I dictate a complete analysis, I fill the personality profile out in far greater detail but at the outset of your experience in astro-analysis, it is much safer to avoid losing the basic topography of a specific personality in a morass of information, or, to go to the other extreme, to find yourself hammering away grimly at one or two points at the expense of the rest. Both are a very common fault among novices and I have even heard of established practitioners falling into such traps.

'My love life's a terrible mess!' Such over-emphasizers on one point wail. 'I've got the Moon square Saturn in my chart!'

Or, on the other hand, you run across the type who complain indignantly, 'How come I always mess up my chances to succeed? I've got the Sun trine Jupiter in my chart!'

In both the above cases, the aspect mentioned has been dragged willy-nilly out of the entire chart pattern, clung to and overstressed to the point that all the other helping or hindering factors therein are virtually ignored.

Perhaps, *the* most important rule in synthesis is: *Look at the impartial personality picture the chart provides as a whole.*

To use another analogy: Look at the chart as a very intricately woven tapestry of traits and potentials. They must *all* be there to make the tapestry what it is. So don't concentrate your gaze on either the brightest or the blackest threads. Look always at the entire tapestry.

SYNTHESIS IN PRACTICE

Right, turn back now to John Jones' completed chart. What does it look like? Not too tough, really. More solid (easy aspects) lines than broken (challenging aspect) lines. What about the categories? One is unproblematical. The other two show marked imbalances — too much negativity: too little fire and air stress. Angular houses? Three out of four occupied by planets. Not going to be one of those jogtrot existences for John Jones! There's the Ascendant playing tug-o-war with the Sun, too.

These initial comments are just by way of gathering a quick impression, of picking up the 'feel' of the chart. But they do tell us at a glance that John Jones is going to have to master major problems in several life sectors to achieve fulfilment of his talents and satisfaction from his life.

This does not mean that we begin by taking a negative, discouraging view in either interpretation or counselling. In my view, each analyst must learn to accentuate the positive in a chart, pointing out potentials (perhaps unrealized), encouraging personal growth, offering hope and development—without, of course, sounding over-optimistic.

Naturally, we must avoid the pitfall of informing clients 'they're wonderful people who are going to have lovely lives'. (Nobody gets off the hook that easily!)

Yet I once listened to part of an analysis done for a 22-year-old girl in which some unknown astrologer said *ad nauseam*, she 'was a lovely girl, who would have a perfectly lovely life, except for nearly succumbing to a serious lung disease at the age of fifty'. Where he picked up the lung disease bit I haven't a clue; why he picked his 'prophecy' date I can't imagine. But since the dread event was not likely to occur till the twenty-first century, he made sure he wouldn't be handy to question if proved wrong.

In chart interpretation we also have to dodge the other pitfall — handing out a dose of unrelieved 'gloom and doom'. (Everybody's clouds have *some* silver linings!)

Personality Profile

1. Hemisphere emphasis

2. Polarities

3. Triplicities

4. Quadruplicities

5. Angular planets

6. Power point character pattern

7. Love and sex nature

8. Success drives

9. Important aspects

....

....

....

10. Comment summary...

....

....

....

....

Now we'll work through John Jones' personality profile.

1. Hemisphere emphasis
Six planets above the horizon in the extroverted, more career-oriented half of the chart.

Four planets below the horizon in the introverted, more private-life-oriented half of the chart.

John thus has a foot in both worlds. Powerful planetary energies above the horizon urge a drive for achievement. But enough planets are below to ensure he does not promote career satisfaction relentlessly at the expense of his private life.

This attitude respects the inherent needs of his Cancer Sun—the Crab's demand for home, emotional expression and family. So from the Hemisphere emphasis, we can say John is something of the 'universal man' type—his urges spread relatively evenly above and below the dividing line of the horizon.

2. Polarities (Positive/Negative pattern)
Here we do strike a stumbling-block for John. Cancer itself is a negative sign. And the overall negative stress is too heavy, promoting passivity, self-repression, the tendency to suppress his own desires to suit others.

Added to this, the only two planets in positive signs are Jupiter and Uranus. Both planets are well-removed from the personality's immediate structure. Hence both are less likely to offer any marked impetus towards positivity in daily living.

Certainly the Ascendant is in a positive sign. This would give a slightly more extroverted *initial* impression, a more positive overlay. But the polarities score does show John needs to develop, through conscious effort and the self-awareness the chart always offers, better powers of self-expression, more positive responses. Otherwise, as he grows older, he will find he has become something of an unwilling 'doormat', hating and resenting the way others walk over him, building up an inner reservoir of frustration.

3. Triplicities (elements pattern)
Again, John is working against a marked imbalance here. Over-emphasis on the traits of earth and water creates a heavy attitude— too much worrying, trying to plan ahead, trying to find practical answers caused by the strong earth sign planets. Too much emotionalism, vulnerability, over-sensitivity caused by the stressed water sign planets.

With his very low fire score, he's going to find action, spontaneity, enthusiasm pretty hard to engender in his behaviour. With his very low air score, he cannot easily detach from his daily worries and doubts—can't switch off and look at problems through the clearer lens of the intellect.

John thus needs to learn to take a lighter, cooler, brighter look at life and himself. To pull himself up out of the mire that overstress on earth/water signs can create. (Too much earth and water = mud.) That takes real, concentrated effort but it can be done.

4. Quadruplicities (Cardinal-fixed-mutable pattern)
Here, John has a fairly even score, a happier balance. The slight emphasis on fixity would give him greater gut confidence, more capacity to take up a determined stance. Added to this, he does have enough planets stressing cardinal energy to give him a sense of goal while the mutables allow him to handle change, be more flexible than the copy-book Cancer type.

5. Angular planets
Three out of the four angular houses are occupied, so John will have to spread his interests throughout life in a more forceful, more active manner than his Cancer Sun may enjoy.

Neptune in the first increases subtlety in self-expression, hinting at creative skills, but also suggesting some gullibility. Cancer in any event is highly impressionable, aware of the slightest nuance in atmosphere. Neptune won't make that any easier to handle. Intuitions are likely to be strong and often spot-on. (Note Neptune's trine to Mercury.) But John needs to watch Neptune's square to Jupiter. This is not a markedly personal aspect but it does imply John and his money can be more easily parted—a nagging worry to a Cancer type.

For relaxation, music should be important to him.

Libra on the cusp of the first should make him more physically appealing and socially aware. The impression he makes on others concerns him a great deal.

Saturn in the fourth, though well-aspected, does not promise much joy through the home. Childhood conditioning seems to have been hard. Almost certainly parents who did not understand his needs, who forgot Cancer children desperately seek constant reassurance of love, and fear the slightest hint of rejection by their intimates.

This early history will set the scene for John's adult home life, because we tend to repeat (however subtly) the domestic conditions we knew as children. Remember, many people who were unhappy as children heavily repress these unpleasant memories but they need to be dragged out into the light if their curbing influence is to be broken.

This Saturn picture can also force a sometimes unwelcome need to 'grow up quickly' in order to be better able to shield the self from hurts.

Capricorn on the cusp of the fourth should attract John to a home that has a touch of 'the establishment' about it—a home that reflects money and financial status. Those he will seek to share his adult home with are likely to be on the 'proper' side too.

No planet in the seventh suggests that, although most Cancer types prefer legal marriage to more modern varieties in relationships, John is less likely to face his greatest trials and tribulations in the state of matrimony or its equivalent.

Aries on the cusp of the seventh, nevertheless can bring a pushy partner into the life, and inclines John—uncharacteristically for

Cancer—to rush into permanent relationships.

The Sun in the tenth promises some measure of distinction and recognition through profession/occupation in John's life, provided a career that is also emotionally satisfying has been chosen.

Cancer on the cusp of the tenth postulates the desire for work that has a nurturing quality, the desire to help or succour others. The Sun's elevated position in the chart plus Cancer tenacity should work together to aim John's talents in the right direction.

6. Power point character pattern (Ascendant-Sun-Moon blend)

Here, again we see John has a problem to confront. The Ascendant and Sun are in conflicting, incompatible signs, both cardinals. The Moon is a mutable. This structure is not too steady. It is like a hovercraft—all the weight resting on top of a soft, shaky base.

There is a constant fight for expression between the people-oriented, diplomatic, cool demeanour of the Scales and the retiring, emotionally slanted, intense reactions of the Crab. Clearly John is one of those people who are anything but what they seem on casual acquaintance or at first blush. He can appear both confusing to others and confused within himself.

The emotionalism of the Crab Sun receives some support from the Fish Moon, both being water signs, both reacting intuitively. But both are equally disconcerted by the Scales Ascendant, which tries to thrust them into the social scene, the professional hurly-burly which neither of them enjoy.

John will have to learn to identify and isolate the needs of the three of them to end the tension. He requires people and situations that can utilize and polish his Libran smoothness to develop greater detachment and intellectual expertise. He also requires people and situations that can sustain and reflect his Cancer/Pisces emotionalism and receptivity.

If he retreats too much into his private world, Libra will fight back. If he leaps too often into the social whirl, Cancer/Pisces will be depleted of their energies. He has to balance the set of contrary demands.

7. *Love and sex nature*

Here we gauge particularly the combined influence of the Moon (emotional needs), Venus (affectional needs) and Mars (sexual needs). John has these planets in an earth-water mix. Partially compatible in their expectations, not too awkward for the women in his life to comprehend, not startlingly different from his basic Cancer self—all of which is quite a help towards John finding the happiness in personal relationships so vital to Cancer.

His Pisces Moon will take him very much into fantasies and fairy tales as far as his emotional affairs go. Neither is likely to come true on this tough planet of ours, so John is emotionally vulnerable, easily affected, easily imposed upon.

His Taurus Venus is sensual, highly tactile but pretty practical as to what is hoped for in any type of affectional involvement. This Venus energy does not restrict itself to partners only but also shows up in all situations where a caring link exists: family, close friends, children, etc. Of course, Taurus doesn't buy for one instant the Fish Moon's romanticism, which can come as a surprise to those intimate with John.

His Virgo Mars squashes the romanticism of the Moon, too, with a strong dash of the Virgin's puristic and even prudish behaviour, making it very hard indeed for John to 'let go'. This does *not* rob John of passion. It merely sets the standards so high that compromise is close to impossible.

But Taurus and Pisces will tolerate each other's needs quite well as do Virgo and Taurus, so the picture is not hopelessly contrary, as it is in some charts you run across.

The house positions of Moon, Venus and Mars throw further light on John's private life.

The Moon in the sixth suggests he may well show moodiness and carry emotional upsets into the working scene.

Venus in the eighth suggests too much influence from older relatives in childhood as to sexual matters and may also push John to seek a mate who offers him money or status.

Mars in the eleventh suggests a passionate search for love, more forceful behaviour towards friends or lovers.

To summarize: John will demand sensuality and supportiveness from his women, coupled with emotional rapport and sensitivity—not the easiest combination to find!

8. Success drives

Here we measure up particularly the combined influence of Mercury (mentality), Jupiter (opportunities) and Saturn (ambitions). John has these three planets in the water-air-earth mix; thus there is not much cohesion between them.

His Cancer Mercury reinforces the emotionally slanted reactions of the Cancer Sun. Intellectual effort is tenacious in the search for security but thinking is likely to be slower, more intuitive. Moods and emotions show themselves vividly in the way he communicates. He speaks as he feels.

His Aquarius Jupiter introduces a somewhat jarring but nevertheless helpful note, if handled satisfactorily. Opportunities are offered because others sense the added humanitarianism, the ability to expand the natural resources. This can make John sometimes over-idealistic in using opportunities but helps pull him out of his emotional depths.

His Capricorn Saturn is valuable in directing John's ambitions. The planet is in its own sign, so both pull together towards solid, slow achievement. John's grasp of strategy in advancing his aims is virtually instinctive and he is likely to thrust hard towards material gain and recognition for his efforts.

Fanfares of trumpets don't interest John. Gilt-edged security and status do!

Harking back to his Cancer Sun, we recall that Cancer, too, seeks financial security because the sign equates it with emotional security. Hence some back-up to John's ambitions could be anticipated from his Sun.

We also note John's Saturn is well-aspected, so his ambitions are much less likely to drive him into arrogance or self-centredness.

The house positions of Mercury, Jupiter and Saturn indicate where John's urge to succeed is most likely to manifest itself.

Mercury in the ninth turns his mind very much towards travel, involvement with foreign-born or foreign-background colleagues, and the search for the right kind of philosophical approach to life.

The diversifying energy of Mercury will open his mind to learning through exposure to foreign cultures. But, of course, his Cancer Sun is far from being a natural globe-trotter and hence may curb travel possibilities from time to time.

Jupiter in the fifth promises chances to expand through various forms of speculation, a marked attraction to children, and a more optimistic approach to romantic opportunities.

But, John needs to watch all forms of gambling or speculation because of Jupiter's hard aspect to Neptune. John can be deceived on these matters, by himself or by smart operators.

Jupiter here also promises successful children—a satisfying thought for John's family-minded Cancer Sun—and the Aquarian cusp of the fifth should permit him to be a little less over-protective towards them, a little more detached.

Saturn in the fourth suggests John's ambitions have been much affected by parental conditioning in childhood so that he still feels a need to prove himself. At some stage in his life, he may decide to run a business or profession from his home base.

To summarize: John likes to think he knows where he's going but he's not a hundred per cent sure of how he's going to arrive there. The spread of his Success drives is a trifle too wide.

9. Important planetary aspects

The Sun's aspects: Sun aspects indicate the natural thrust of each individual's will, the push towards satisfaction of each life-purpose. They also supply clues to our relationships with men in all roles, commencing with the father and other male authority figures, then later translating themselves into our adult reactions to men as colleagues, intimates, friends. In everyday life, we all benefit from easy Sun aspects: need to watch challenging Sun aspects.

John has favourable aspects to the Sun. There's a trine to Neptune and a sextile to Pluto. The Neptune link will encourage a more subtle, more intuitive response in dealings with males, increasing as well John's charm and creative potential.

The Pluto link offers greater penetration of the motivations of men plus added self-reliance.

Hence, despite the problematical effect of his early home life, we deduce that John has not acquired a damaged image of men that could cause problems in his life.

The Moon's aspects: Moon aspects indicate the natural flow of each individual's emotions, the search for expression of deep inner needs. They also supply clues to our relationships with women in all roles, commencing with the mother and other female authority figures then later translating themselves into our adult reactions to women as colleagues, intimates, friends. In emotional life, we all benefit from easy Moon aspects: need to watch challenging Moon aspects.

John has a mixed bag of aspects to the Moon. There's a square to Mercury and two mildly helpful sextiles to Venus and Saturn. The Mercury aspect is a *hidden* square. (Check aspect chapter again if you don't understand this.) John has problems in verbalizing his emotional needs so that misunderstandings become highly probable. What John *says* about his feelings/needs is not often what his intimates *hear*. Quite a hurdle for emotional Cancer types. John must work hard on surmounting this difficulty.

The Venus link offers some assistance in obviating misunderstandings, a better tuning in to the responses of females in John's life.

The Saturn link allows John to come to terms with his own emotional expectations, making him stronger and more supportive than his Piscean Moon would otherwise imply.

Mercury's aspects: Mercury aspects reveal the hindering or helping by planetary energies of our mental development, communicative and intellectual skills.

In mental life we all benefit from easy Mercury aspects: need to watch challenging Mercury aspects.

John has some favourable additional aspects to Mercury. There's a trine to Neptune, two mildly helpful sextiles to Mars and Pluto.

The Neptune link steps up capacity for imaginative, even inspired thinking. Also the ability to grasp intangibles with ease.

The Mars link boosts mental energy, although some premature

jumping to conclusions needs to be restrained.

The Pluto link develops a greater depth of thought, and greater gut-level insight.

Venus' aspects: Venus aspects provide clues to what we hope for in love and friendship and whether planetary energies will assist or misdirect such hopes. In love-life, we all benefit from easy Venus aspects: need to watch challenging Venus aspects.

John has a mixed bag of additional aspects to Venus. There are trines to Jupiter and Saturn, squares to Mars and Uranus.

The link with Jupiter allows greater popularity in personal life because it triggers a broader, more generous response.

The link with Saturn adds strength and further supportiveness in affectional involvements. A capacity to sacrifice his own needs for those cared about clearly exists.

The link with Mars (another hidden aspect) presents John with real problems, urging him into intense attractions, possible infatuations, which will set him back on his heels in a mood of anger, truculence and frustration. He needs to restrain this since he is very open to hurt as we've already noted.

The link with Uranus hurls a spanner into his affectional life with electric force. John is pulled by it like a steel to a magnet towards unconventional, off-beat, unreliable types as friends and/or lovers. It further sets up fear of lasting commitments, makes him prize too highly his personal space.

This one is really bad news for John's Cancer Sun. Taken aback, shocked and frightened by this wild, alien demand which can rear up suddenly like a monster from the depths, the Sun struggles desperately to control it, knowing only too well that it will create the type of unstable, even dangerous relationships Cancer instinctively dreads. Thus John will need to hold this demand firmly in check, choosing his intimates with the utmost care.

Mars' aspects: Mars aspects point to the uses we find for our physical and sexual energies and indicate whether planetary energies will employ or squander both. In physical living, we all benefit from easy Mars aspects: need to watch challenging Mars aspects.

John has some favourable additional aspects to Mars. There is a conjunction to Pluto and a sextile to Neptune.

The link with Pluto promotes tremendous physical drives, originating in the subconscious mind, triggering the quest for power and conquest, ensuring that sexual repressions will not hamper sexual satisfaction. But it also introduces a competitive push which is not too comfortable for the Cancer Sun.

The link with Neptune, much milder, again adds subtlety allowing John to sense what his partner requires in lovemaking.

This one is much easier for John's Cancer Sun to handle because it also promotes benefit from the sea. And most water sign people have a natural affinity for water, gaining both physical and spiritual replenishment therefrom.

Comments on personality profile preparation

We now see we have discovered a great deal about John Jones in all life sectors, in both his personal and public environment. We see him as a complete person and we know him better than his oldest friends and closest family. We may even know him better through the medium of the chart than he knows himself!

We can isolate his strengths and his weaknesses. If we were counselling him, we would show him how to prevent the minuses in his chart — the tough aspects, the imbalances — from damaging his achievement potential. We would also encourage him to maximize his assets — the easy aspects, the strong practical streak, the imaginative powers — to make his goals easier to attain.

From then on, the ball is in John Jones' court, as it is in everyone's. Carl Jung, the great psychoanalyst and renowned astrologer, always stressed this point—that in counselling others, the analyst can only give guidelines. He must not and cannot take over the other person's life.

Remember, too, that although through the bulk of this chapter we've been discussing a specific male we've called John Jones, we've also been learning something more about everyone who shares any of his patterns and aspects.

We've observed the process of synthesis in action and discovered many of the secrets of personality that the horoscope chart reveals. Naturally, what I have set out here is a simplified set of steps in synthesis. I take many more factors into consideration to round out a personality profile but attempting to tie in too much is disastrously confusing to beginners. It won't help your confidence if you wind up with masses of contrary information that seems to lead in all directions at once. So do take synthesis slowly. Build the foundation. Prepare the outline of the structure before you begin adding trimmings. After all, you can't hang pictures in a new house till you've got the walls up. The same applies to chart synthesis.

To check your progress with synthesis, it's always fascinating to attempt an analysis of a chart of some famous individual. You can check your own conclusions more easily because the lives of most public figures are well-known through newspapers, magazines and biographies. If you wish to try this, you will of course need your 'Tools of the Trade' set out earlier. You can't begin general chart erection work without your ephemeris, house tables, atlas, daylight saving book and time zone information—at the very least.

However, assuming you have these, here are some famous people and their accompanying birth data.

Prince Charles of England: Born 9.14 p.m. on 14.11.48 in London, England.

Princess Diana, his wife: Born 7.45 p.m. on 1.7.61 in Sandringham, Norfolk, England.

Prince William, their first child: Born 9.02 p.m. on 21.6.82 in London, England.

Former US President Richard Nixon: Born 9.1.13 at 9.44 p.m. in Yorba Linda, California, USA.

Film star Marilyn Monroe: Born 1.6.26 at 9.09 a.m. in Los Angeles, California, USA.

Predictably, the charts of the above have been analysed and re-analysed by top astrologers all over the world, so as a further check you'll find their interpretations in astrology texts by leading authors. Compare and decide how your findings stand up to those of the experts!

While you're considering these charts, ask yourself why:

(a) Prince Charles often gives a somewhat ambivalent impression in public appearances;
(b) Princess Diana is speedily revealing herself as a thoroughly modern, 'new wave' type of woman;
(c) former president Nixon got the nickname of 'Tricky Dicky';
(d) Marilyn Monroe couldn't handle her role as America's sex goddess.

The charts of these four contain the answers. See if you can discover them.

THE 'HEADLINER-HUNTING' GAME

Looking for a fast and fun way of sharpening up your skills in the science of chart interpretation? Then try playing 'Hunt the Headliner!' Here's how to start:

1. Make a short list of famous historical figures whose lives interest you, choosing those who have made history *often!*
2. Take a trip to your local library and hunt up everything you can about your listed personalities—biographies, autobiographies, etc., gathering birthdates and (if possible) birthtimes. Comprehensive encyclopaedias are an invaluable source of information too. Yet another source is to be found in the various astrological texts which contain ready-prepared charts of world figures. (But check the author here! There are heaps of trashy astrology books around whose writers make mind-boggling blunders in chart calculation, birthdates and everything else.)
3. Make notes on each individual on your list till you have what we psychologists call a *personality profile* for each one from the data you've collected in your reading (i.e. setting out notable characteristics, typical behaviour patterns, mental attitudes, responses to love, friendship, etc.).
4. Erect a chart yourself for your 'headliners'—solar if you cannot obtain birthtime or doubt its accuracy.
5. Compare what your analysis of their charts reveals with the life-style and life-story of all your 'headliners'.

This little 'game' is the best way I know for students to stack up their analytical skills against the facts of life. And, that's why I suggest you choose exceptionally famous people. Because every small detail in their lives is well-documented, having been examined and picked over by authors, journalists and historians.

Even if you have no birthtime, the solar chart will still indicate the important planetary positions and aspects, the Sun-Moon blend and what notable planetary configurations exist.

Should you discover your analysis doesn't quite fit with the facts, start again. You, not astrological deduction, will have slipped up somewhere because, in my view, the chart is never wrong when correctly and meticulously interpreted.

You should be able to see why your chosen 'headliner' hit the tops in fame or notoriety, why they chose the lovers/spouses they did, how they reaped the benefits of their success or were destroyed by it. Some 'headliners' you'll observe instinctively followed the talents shown in their chart. American vocational guidance consultant Charles Luntz cited this type of case with the original Rockefeller multi-millionaire, whose powerfully placed Neptune led him towards the then-burgeoning oil industry. This instinct raised Rockefeller from a lowly sales clerk to the ranks of the richest and most powerful men in the world!

Other 'headliners', like the pathetic Judy Garland, rocketed to fame early in their lives but lacked the strength to survive it. Again, the chart will tell you why.

It is intriguing too, when reading fiction in which world figures feature, to watch how the author handles them and how many of their chart characteristics appear.

I recently waded through that massive tome by Herman Wouk— *The Winds of War*—which was also televised in some countries. The story itself I thought rather boring, but the portraits of Roosevelt, Hitler, Churchill, Stalin and Mussolini reflected their horoscope traits so vividly that I wondered if Wouk had some knowledge of astrology. That was not very likely, I concluded, which proved perhaps even more clearly how individuals conform to their birth patterns. Some of Wouk's comments on the protagonists of World War Two could have come straight out of astrological textbooks on Sun-sign traits. Roosevelt was an Aquarian, Hitler a Taurean, Churchill a Sagittarian, Mussolini a Leo, and Stalin a Capricorn.

If you'd like to try your hand at interpreting by constructing solar charts for the famous or notorious five—their dates as given in most reference works in birth order are as follows:

Churchill.................30 November 1874
Stalin ....2 January 1880
Roosevelt.................30 January 1882
Mussolini ....29 July 1883
Hitler ....20 April 1889

Even from merely looking at their birthdates, a few intriguing facts emerge.

Churchill was 14½ years older than Hitler, so their generation planets and hence their gut reactions would have to be very different, some by sign and some by a wide divergence in degree.

The oldest pair, Churchill and Stalin, outlived the rest by more than a decade. Sagittarius is a vigorously physical sign; Capricorn is very durable.

Roosevelt, Churchill and Stalin all died from illnesses. Mussolini was executed and Hitler shot himself.

Hitler was the only one of the five born on a cusp; right on the dividing line between Aries and Taurus but technically a Taurean, the Sun being at 0 degrees 48 minutes on his day of birth. (His world conquest aims plus his lifelong passion for building and architecture neatly express the twin demands of Aries and Taurus.)

All were men born into the social conditions and mental attitudes of the nineteenth century yet their decisions changed the lives of countless millions of twentieth-century-born individuals.

Food for thought when you line the facts up, isn't it? And you'll find much more of the same to test your skills and prove the great truths of astrology when you start your own 'headliner-hunting' game!

By the way, if you wish to work on charts for 'headliners' who were born anywhere in time before the decade beginning with 1890, you'll need to buy or borrow books which contain prepared charts of top names. Most astrological societies or federations of

astrologers in various countries have these and often own copies
of the ephemeris which cover earlier centuries. You cannot buy
ephemeris before 1890 in most astrology bookshops but some
books of prepared charts go back to individuals born as long ago
as Julius Caesar.

Another fascinating discovery you'll make from working with
charts of the famous is this. Very often you'll find the personalities
who appeal most to you have charts compatible with your own.
I recall one of my clients, a leading architect, once said to me:
'Whenever I'm uncertain or depressed I always play something
by Beethoven. It's almost uncanny. The man seems to speak to
me through his music.'

Sure enough, I checked out Beethoven's chart and the great
composer's Mercury (communication and mentality) was in an
exact conjunction with my client's. Beethoven *was* speaking to my
client and had they lived at the same time, they could have
communicated easily with each other.

On the other hand, you'll discover with this type of chart
investigatory work you can feel greater sympathy and
understanding for famous individuals you *didn't* much fancy.

I remember once I was preparing a lecture on the late Elvis Presley
(whom I did like) and ran into biographical comment on his
admiration for the late James Dean (whom I never liked). This
spurred me to set up the chart of that controversial film-star of
the 1950s. At once, it could be seen why Presley admired him *and*
why Dean behaved in the erratic, unorthodox manner that he did.
For those students who'd like to try working with Presley and Dean,
their birth data is as follows:

Elvis Presley was born at Tupelo, Mississippi, USA, at 4.35 a.m.
on 8 January 1935 (see later).

James Dean was born at Marion, Indiana, USA at 9.09 p.m. on
8 February 1931.

A meeting with Mozart

To show you in greater detail how improving your interpretative
skills is boosted by studying charts of famous historical
personalities, let's arrange an introduction to Wolfgang Amadeus

Mozart—Austria's greatest musical genius, via his horoscope chart.

I myself wanted very much to get to know him better after seeing that excellent stage play about his extraordinary life which was entitled *Amadeus*.

From the first appearance on stage of the actor portraying Mozart, every professional astrologer in the audience would have had to suspect Mozart could not have been anything else *but* an Aquarian. He surely was, and he always played the role fortissimo! With good reason. No less than four planets in the sign of the Water-Bearer plus (Heaven help him!) a Virgo Ascendant and a Sagittarian Moon.

Not being the madly musical type myself, I had never thought seriously about Mozart until the revelations of his character in the play started me off on an astro-historical search for the answers. The results were fascinating. I checked the basic facts of his short life in encyclopaedias and obtained his birth data from astrological reference works. Born in Salzburg, Austria at 8 p.m. on 27 January 1756.

Check for yourself from Mozart's chart in this section and note the following pointers: Loaded fifth house of creativity with Sun, Mercury and Saturn all there in Aquarius. Venus, also Aquarius, in sixth. Uranus in Pisces in seventh. Mars in Cancer in tenth. Moon and Pluto in fourth in Sagittarius. Neptune in Leo in eleventh. Jupiter in Libra in second. (Check over, now, Mozart's chart in this section and note down your own conclusions before reading further.)

Even more intriguing, the author of *Amadeus* allowed his hero to display just about every trait shown in the natal chart, in all its eccentric glory. (I wonder if an astrologer interpreted it for him beforehand?) Among the choicer morsels of Aquarian unconventionality, aided and abetted by the Sagittarian Moon, was Mozart's leaping on his chosen damsel in full evening dress on the library carpet during a soirée at the mansion of a close and aristocratic friend of the Austrian Emperor. (He had gone to the party, hoping to attract a little of the royal cash!!!)

Another morsel, this time with the Virgo Ascendant in full cry as well, was Mozart's announcement, complete with gales of raucous laughter, to the court composer that the said dignitary's latest march was a masterpiece of mistakes. (Mozart had approached him hoping to attract a spot of official sponsorship!)

Pluto in the House of the Home and Uranus in the House of Marriage had their accustomed fun in creating domestic upheavals, weird hangups about his chequered infant prodigy childhood, sudden marital trauma, etc.

Mars in the House of Career ensured he would wave the fiery sword when his contemporaries failed to understand his musical genius, brilliant, ahead-of-his-time innovations and his penchant for glorifying ordinary people in his operas.

The unstable emotional picture (Moon square Uranus, amongst other things) scarcely needed to add to the bohemian contempt for convention. Not to mention the fantasy-generating oppositions between the Sun, Mercury and Neptune.

Perpetually penniless, always misinterpreted, Mozart's tragic and inevitable end was death in obscurity on 5 December 1791 at the age of thirty-six—a sad finish for a man whose musical genius was so revolutionizing and so extraordinary that five short piano pieces he composed at the *age of four* are still frequently played today!

The play gave the official cause of death as kidney failure, hastened by exposure to freezing conditions. (He didn't even have the price of a load of firewood!) The encyclopaedias give it as typhoid fever. Again, his chart offers some clues. Aries on the House of Death certainly implies the possibility of fever and sudden infection as the cause of demise. Libra, traditional ruler of the kidney area, on the House of Money with Jupiter posited therein hints at a less obvious reason for untimely death: the hope for ease and equilibrium in financial affairs (Libra), the promise of great opportunities for wealth (Jupiter), both perhaps instinctively felt yet both unrealized. The injustice of seeing mediocrity richly rewarded and genius summarily dismissed could well have been the final straw that broke the camel's back.

After seeing *Amadeus*, and then analysing Mozart's chart, I think any biographer of historical figures would be well-advised to have a chart erected for his/her subject. It contains the answers to all the riddles of human personality and swiftly turns the cardboard effigies of history into living, breathing people.

Mozart's Natal Chart

Cardinal signs 2   Name: Wolfgang Amadeus Mozart   FIRE signs   3
Fixed signs   5   AIR signs   5
Mutable signs   3   EARTH signs 0
Positive signs 8   B. Salzburg, Austria   WATER signs 2
Negative signs 2   S. Placidean

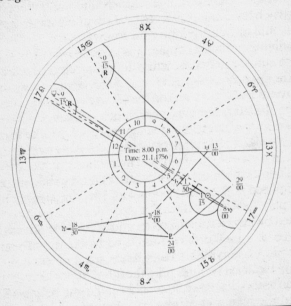

B.T.Q.	Planet	Natal	Major Aspects
P F F	11 ♆ Neptune	9.15 ♌ **R**	
N M W	7 ♅ Uranus	13.00 ♓	
P F A	5 ♄ Saturn	1.50 ♒	☍ ♆
P C A	2 ♃ Jupiter	18.30 ♎	✳ ♇
N C W	10 ♂ Mars	0.15 ♋ **R**	⊼ ♄
P F A	10 ☉ Sun	7.15 ♒	♂ ☿ ♂ ♄ ☍ ♆
P F A	6 ♀ Venus	29.00 ♒	✳ ♇ △ ♂
P F A	5 ☿ Mercury	8.00 ♒	♂ ♄ ☍ ♆
P M F	4 ☽ Moon	18.00 ♐	♂ ♇ ✳ ♃ □ ♅
P M F	4 ♇ Pluto	24.00 ♐	

THE ENIGMA OF ELVIS

Love him or hate him . . . Rubbish him or rave about him . . . Unless you're under 10 or over 100, you won't be asking 'Elvis who?'.

For Elvis—the legendary King of Rock 'n' Roll—became, in a very brief span of years, the most universally famous human being on earth! The only face more familiar than his anywhere in the world is that of Mickey Mouse!

Staggered to read a statement like that? So was I when I began former English Literature Professor and top music critic Albert Goldman's massive 720-page biography of popular music's greatest name.

Every page I turned produced another shock, another astonishing insight into a personality so enigmatic, so paradoxical that if Goldman's book was a work of fiction you simply wouldn't believe a word of it.

Naturally, this set me off in search of the astrological answers to the fame and tragedy which pursued Elvis throughout his adult life.

To begin with, I wondered precisely what had stimulated a man of Goldman's intellectual stature to research, in such relentless detail, the rise and fall of an individual whom most academics dismissed as a dumb, hill-billy freak.

By the time I was only a few pages into the biography, I had found the reason. Elvis *was* an extraordinary human being. Charismatic yet contrary, violent yet docile, flamboyant yet timid . . . you run out of contradictory adjectives when you try to describe him.

Let's list some of the remarkable facts of his life (as Goldman relates them) up to his sudden death somewhere after 8 a.m. and before 2 p.m. on 16 August 1977.

Then let's see how the facts stack up against the dominant planetary patterns which appear in Elvis' horoscope chart.

Our first step in our journey into the psyche of Elvis rings an immediate warning bell and at the same time, yet again, proves that painstaking astrological deduction *never* gives wrong answers.

The warning is summed up in the old adage . . . 'Look before you leap' . . . especially if you're planning to leap into print.

In Chapter 4, page 86, Albert Goldman, writing on Elvis' birth and family background states: 'It is highly characteristic of the mentality of Elvis Presley's millions of fans and numerous hagiographers that none of them ever thought to verify the story by seeking out appropriate records.'

Goldman did just that. He checked the records of the physician who attended the birth and found an entry in the doctor's 'baby book' which stated that at 4.00 a.m. on 8 January 1935, Mrs Gladys Presley was delivered of a stillborn son. At 4.35 a.m. she had another son, who survived.

This birth-time revelation is only one of many 'spanners' that Goldman throws into the works as he sets about demolishing the myths which surround and obscure the real Elvis.

For anyone who has examined Elvis' chart in magazines or textbooks will recall that most authors/biographers assign a *noon birth time* to him, thus tagging him with a Taurus Ascendant. *The correct 4.35 a.m. time gives a Sagittarian Ascendant.*

And this proves the second point I mentioned above. Until I began the Goldman biography, I hadn't paid much attention to Elvis although I did remember he was supposed to have a Taurus Ascendant.

Yet the more I read about him, the more I began to feel that Taurus Rising wasn't right, didn't explain Elvis at all. Little clues through the text kept niggling at me . . . the divide in his front teeth, the fairish hair, the confusing behaviour so typical of clashes between the Ascendant-Sun-Moon blend.

'What?' I hear all the Elvis fans out there protesting. 'Elvis had no gap in his teeth and his hair was blue-black!'

Not so, Goldman reveals. The gap was there alright but Elvis hated it, had a dentist fix it out of some of the first pay he earned as a truckie.

(*Note:* A gap in the front teeth is a common indicator of a Sagittarian Ascendant.)

As for the blue-black hair, *that* wasn't natural either. It came out of a bottle, partially to satisfy Elvis' adolescent urge to emulate handsome actor Tony Curtis. Partially to defeat the Presley family failing of early greying. Indeed, were it not for the ever-present dye bottle, Goldman reports, Elvis would have been grey as the proverbial badger in his early thirties.

(*Note:* Light to chestnut-tinged hair is usual with a Sagittarian Ascendant.)

Add these two important little clues to what Goldman described as 'Elvis' wire-strung soul' which would begin to jangle at the slightest stimulus, and you'd have to diagnose powerful clashes between the power points of Elvis' chart.

Thus when his true birth-time was revealed on page 86 of the Goldman book, you'd only have to calculate the chart to see all the loose ends which never blended with a Taurus Ascendant tie neatly into place.

All of which should serve as a reminder that in any astrological research, we should continue checking our sources till we arrive at those which are based on unassailable evidence. For if your facts are wrong, so will be your deductions and this may bring ridicule the science of astrology does not deserve.

Major planetary indicators in Elvis' chart

To save space and because I consider it easier for newcomers to astrology to follow, I'll set out hereafter Elvis' major planetary aspects and planetary positions instead of including the chart in diagrammatic form.

Next, we'll see how these reflect some more of Goldman's shattering revelations about Elvis' personality and life style.

Ascendant = Sagittarius: Sun = Capricorn, 2nd house: Moon = Pisces, 3rd house: Mercury = Capricorn, 2nd house: Mars = Libra, 10th house: Jupiter = Scorpio, 12th house: Saturn = Aquarius, 3rd house, Uranus = Aries, 5th house: Neptune = Virgo, 9th house: Pluto = Cancer, 8th house. (*Note:* Both Moon and Venus are close to cusp of Aquarius.)

Major Aspects: Personal Planets

Sun favourable Mercury, Neptune and Jupiter. Sun unfavourable Mars. Mercury favourable Venus, Neptune and Jupiter. Mercury unfavourable Uranus and Pluto. Venus unfavourable Uranus and Pluto.

(*Note:* The Moon is fairly close to a conjunction with Saturn but has no other major aspects; Mars has no further major aspects other than the Sun/Mars link mentioned above.)

Categories:
Strong negative stress: Strong cardinal stress: Strong earth/water stress, low scores on air/fire.

So much for the pointers in Elvis' chart: now we'll match them up with Goldman's information, gleaned from scores of interviews with just about every living person who'd had close contact with the Rock King, in and out of his Graceland palace.

● Elvis saw himself as a divinely-appointed Messenger, Master or Chosen One. Identified his sudden and incredible success as evidence of divine, not merely mortal favour. In his last years, he appeared on stage, illuminated by blazing searchlights, to the thundering sound of heavenly music, clad in white and gleaming with so many jewels . . . the image was that of a supernatural being.

Astro-comment: Moon in Pisces is adept at producing emotionally-based fantasies. The proximity to Aquarius adds the conviction of superiority. Neptune close to the Mid-Heaven mixes in the religious fervour.

● Elvis was capable of lunatic extravagance and pinch-penny meanness all at once. He paid his close associates tiny wages yet thought nothing of buying them costly cars by the dozen. He once spent more than 16,000 dollars on a night flight in his private plane across America to treat his mates to a special variety of jelly sandwiches!

Astro-comment: Mercury (mentality) and Venus (affections) both show hard aspects to Uranus and Pluto. Both sets of aspects create disturbing behaviour. Erratic yet compulsive thinking on the one hand: desperate desire for love and popularity, coupled with sudden switch-offs.

● Elvis' strange relationship with his exceedingly strange mother was tormented and tortuous. When she died in August 1958, the 23-year-old chief mourner clung so fiercely to the coffin as it was being lowered into the grave, it took the combined heaving of several men to pry him loose. Goldman adds that Gladys Presley's death was a deadly wound from which Elvis never recovered and led to the horrifying drug dependence throughout his later years.

Astro-comment: The Moon's proximity to Saturn hints at the mother as a Saturnine authority figure, boosting self-confidence at the price of total dependency. Once she was gone, Elvis had to find these instinctual needs elsewhere. The presence of the Moon in Pisces, but posited in the 3rd house in company with Saturn plus the self-indulgent Jupiter in the 12th house (self-undoing) suggest the possibility of Elvis' search ending in the fantasy world of drugs. In his last years, the dream world finally ousted the real one. Elvis would lie for days in a drugged stupor while his lovers cooed and cuddled him as if he had in fact returned to babyhood.

● Elvis' much-publicised refusal to give concert tours outside the United States was not the singer's idea but his manager's . . . that weird and wonderful creature known as Colonel Tom Parker. Goldman reveals that neither the title, the name, nor the 'Colonel's' claim to American nationality were genuine. Goldman asserts that Parker was Dutch-born, had entered America by mysterious means and hence never wanted to take the risk of applying for a passport. This refusal of overseas tours apparently lost Elvis millions of dollars.

Astro-comment: Here is Neptune in the 9th up to his old tricks, producing peculiar blocks to travel, leaving Elvis' mind open to manipulation by those of foreign background. It is equally interesting to note that the 'Colonel' organized Elvis' induction into the U.S. army to serve in Germany for reasons that were senseless and spurious. This experience of army life undermined Elvis' always shaky self-confidence to the point that it virtually disappeared. At this period, too, he first encountered Priscilla, his future wife and thus became embroiled in a strange entanglement that was damaging to both parties. The whole scene was dangerously Neptunian.

● Elvis' avowed admiration for and brief association with actor James Dean . . . that cult figure of the 1950s . . . puzzled his friends and his biographer. How could Elvis (whose politeness towards

the famous was punctilious to the point of becoming excruciating)
think so highly of another young performer whose behaviour was
the antithesis of his own? Few, says Goldman, could outdo Elvis
in the stream of 'Yes, Sirs' and 'Yes, Ma'ams' that accompanied
introductions. Dean, on the other hand, was wont to greet the great
with a stream of four-letter words.

Astro-comment: Although Dean was an Aquarian with Libra
Ascendant and Scorpio Moon, he shared with Elvis a T-Square
Planetary Configuration in Cardinal signs. In each case Pluto and
Uranus were part of the 'T'. Dean's Mercury (mentality) was in
a close conjunction with Elvis' Mercury . . . both in the third
decanate of Capricorn. This mental link pattern always promotes
easier communication between two individuals. Both Dean and
Elvis had the Mercury Opposition Pluto aspect which often creates
a sense of personal futility. Both had Mars in the 10th house,
implying an almost militant desire for fame and career recognition.
Elvis who liked to break the 'rules' in private was doubtless
impressed by Dean's Aquarian ability to break them in public.

● Elvis loudly and often denounced every variety of drug-taker
or 'Junkie'. Yet at his death, he weighed 18 stone (114 kg) and the
autopsy revealed no less than fourteen different drugs, including
one at a concentration ten times higher than the toxic level. Added
to this astonishing contradiction, Elvis' most prized badge (and
he collected badges of authority like some collect stamps) was that
of a fully-fledged federal narcotics agent . . . a favour he received
at his own request from fellow Capricorn, U.S. President Nixon.

Astro-comment: Elvis' talent for reconciling the irreconcilable in
this mind-boggling manner and his fearsome weight problem have
several sources in his chart. His Sagittarian Ascendant constantly
rushed him headlong into situations his Capricorn Sun did not
like and couldn't handle. The unending glare of publicity, the
inability to give anything but his best to his fans placed horrifying
strains on body, mind and soul. The only answer his Pisces Moon
could offer was the escape of drugs and the 'consolation' of over-
eating. Naturally, the somewhat self-righteous attitudes of
Sagittarius plus the propriety of Capricorn would not allow any
conscious admission of his failings. The solution was Neptunian

in the extreme. Elvis convinced himself his drugs were only necessary medication . . . obtaining them through medical prescriptions by dubious means. The fantasy element of Neptune was prominent in his over-eating as well. Much of his favourite 'nibbles' were kindergarten treats. It was nothing for him to send his valet out in the middle of the night to buy $100's worth of the U.S. version of 'lollipops' . . . again evidencing the imaginary retreat to the safer world of childhood.

Lastly, here are a few further flashes of insight into the psyche of Elvis:

● Despite his wildly sexual public image, Elvis was a maniacal sermonizer, reading religious books by the barrow-load and lecturing his henchmen on Life and God through the long watches of the night. (Sagittarius Ascendant again, Neptune in 9th.)

● Despite the fact that the world's women from the most glamorous sex goddesses of Hollywood to the plainest home town girls fell at his feet, Elvis constantly doubted his own sex appeal and gained little satisfaction from his endless love affairs. (Venus in hard aspect to Uranus and Pluto.)

● Despite the fact that he could become painfully timorous in face-to-face confrontations with authority figures, Elvis maintained a veritable armoury of weapons about his person to shoot up television sets and anything else which annoyed him. In his later years, Elvis' valet regularly slipped blanks into his master's pistols to prevent him from shooting up people. (Sun in hard aspect to Mars: Aries on 5th, Uranus in 5th.)

The foregoing are only random scraps from the Goldman biography. The comments too are necessarily brief. It would take a book as big as Goldman's to explain Elvis astrologically . . . all the labrynthine twists and turns in this amazing personality . . . whose 'voice of electric honey' still sings around the world and whose glittering image remains undimmed.

Perhaps the best epitaph to Elvis came from the lips of the dread Colonel Parker, who, when told of his 'boy's' death said: 'Nothing has changed. This won't change anything.' It didn't either. Elvis was dead — but only physically!

This article first appeared in *Astrological Monthly Review* Vol 46, No. 13, in January 1984.

8.

BECOMING AN EFFECTIVE ASTRO-ANALYST

A CODE OF ETHICS

I thought we'd start this concluding chapter with a short homily on precisely what being a good chart analyst adds up to. Whether you're interested in the science only as an absorbing hobby or you have intentions of qualifying as a practitioner, sooner or later (usually sooner) someone is going to ask you for advice. And here—as Shakespeare said—is the rub! Here's the awesome responsibility you have to pick up and carry. Because people aren't asking you whether they should buy a new outfit or have steak for lunch. *People are asking you to help them in running their lives!*

No one ever described this responsibility better than Hippocrates, the great Greek physician-astrologer, who formulated the Hippocratic Oath of service to humanity still sworn by doctors today. That fact is well-known. Rather less known is the further fact that Hippocrates also formulated an oath for astrologers. I'll quote it in its entirety hereunder in the manner set out by Nicholas de Vore in his *Encyclopedia of Astrology*. Here's the Hippocratic Oath. Digest it and abide by it and you'll be serving your science faithfully and well.

I will not give 'readings', 'tell fortunes', or make predictions to satisfy the morbid cravings of the curious, nor will I seek to astound or mystify; but will give consultations only to those who have a problem regarding which they know they need help and seek it; and instead of prophesying a prognosis, I will endeavor to instill the right thinking that will contribute to avoiding or mitigating an unfavorable condition which I see in operation, interpreting such in terms of influences rather than of events, and at all times teaching a philosophy of Free Will and emotional self-control that is the antithesis of Fatalism and Predestination.

I will not give counsel contrived to assist any person in working injury to or taking unfair advantage of another.

I will never make an utterance or inference that will reflect in any degree upon any other practitioner; nor will I treat a client of another practitioner, except as called in consultation by such practitioner.

I will never relax in my efforts to add to my knowledge of the science, to impart it to such as I deem worthy to follow in my footsteps, and to devote my efforts without stint toward the improving of human understandings and personal relationships, and in rendering service to humanity and society.

And may the Creator who placed the planets in their orbits as His means of guiding the Destinies of men, preserve and sustain me in proportion to the fidelity with which I exemplify the laws I am ordained to teach.

Hippocrates didn't pull any punches, did he? What's more, he delivered a knock-out blow to those who would drag astrology down into a fortune-telling device. And he landed another hit on those who nurture the mediaeval notion that astrology is some variety of black magic.

His last paragraph raises another point of enormous significance: the personal integrity of the analyst. I feel this means we all must look to our own motivations for studying and possibly practising astrology. If we have turned to it in a sincere and genuine search for greater self-awareness, a greater understanding of the purpose of life, then we are on the right path. If, on the other hand, we have turned to astrology as an ego trip (i.e. to astound and mystify friends) or to acquire power and control over others (i.e. to take an unfair advantage), then we are very definitely on the wrong path.

The law of gravity states that what goes up must come down. The law of karma states that what we give out must come back to us. Hence if you give the best of yourself to your science, you will be rewarded with the best of results. The knowledge that you have helped others along the obstacle course of life will help you to grow spiritually and mentally.

In short: 'Do unto others as you would have them do unto you.' That is the way Jesus Christ put it. And, it is important to observe here, that true astrology has never had any quarrel with established religions or the Christian Church.

Indeed, true astrology constantly reveals divine power in the intricate tapestry of virtues and vices each chart represents—all of which are designed to test us and help us evolve to the utmost of our capacities, and none of which could have occurred by chance or accident.

The self-knowledge the chart offers was thus never intended to weaken the will or to delude us into thinking that we are mere pawns of capricious fate, but to act as a guiding light, showing us where our inadequacies lie and offering us the strength to overcome them.

I make this point emphatically since many students do sometimes worry that their interest in astrology will cause havoc with their religious convictions.

An American astrologer, who warned the late President Kennedy not to drive through Dallas on that fateful November day in 1963, summed up the astrology v. religion controversy very aptly. Kennedy is reported to have answered her warning with, 'I put my faith in God, not in the stars.' To which she replied: 'And Who, Mr President, do you think made the stars?'

FURTHER AREAS OF INVESTIGATION

In a concise course such as this, we cannot cover the many other fields in which astrology can guide and assist you. *Synastry*—the comparison of two charts to judge compatibility in love or business— is one very important field which I plan to deal with in a later book. *Future life trends* represents another area of investigation which has not been included here because, in my view, any form of forecasting should not be attempted until you are fully competent in analysing the natal chart.

In any event, the natal chart contains numerous future potentials in all life sectors. Further, influences exerted by planetary transits or progressions *never* operate as separate energies. They can only activate or baulk what is shown in the natal chart itself. This, of course, is yet another reason why the so-called 'forecasts' which appear in the popular press are pure 'fairy floss'—even in cases where they claim to be based on more than the twelve Sun signs.

Countless people will exhibit similar future aspects at a given time, but because each natal chart is as unique as a thumbprint, each individual will handle both the opportunities and setbacks implied by transiting or progressing planets in a different manner.

Just as with natal chart potentials, some individuals are strong enough to make molehills out of mountains of problems and turn certain defeat into total victory. Others will be thrown way off course by the slightest obstacle, the merest hint of trouble.

BASIC LIBRARY REQUIREMENTS

If you wish to be a good astro-analyst you'll need to read widely and watch new research, but many texts are costly and hard to come by. Hence the books in the short list that follows are available in paperback and all by highly qualified authors. The only expensive work listed is Margaret Hone's, which is well worth buying because of the additional data it contains on time zones and daylight saving.

Technical-type astrology texts are only obtainable at specialist astrology bookshops.

You can't get by without your 'Tools of the Trade', fully set out in our Chapter 5. These include: Planetary Ephemeris Atlas, Houses Tables, Zone and Standard Time Lists, Daylight Saving Data (none of them expensive).

You'll extend your knowledge with:

The Modern Textbook of Astrology Margaret Hone (Fowler, 1978).

Encyclopedia of Astrology Nicholas de Vore (Litlefield, Adams, 1980).

Time Changes in the World Doris Chase Doane. (Her two other time changes books are also necessary if you want to erect charts for people born in Canada and the United States.)

Teach Yourself Astrology Jeff Mayo (Hodder, 1964).

Astrology, Psychology and the Four Elements Stephen Arroyo, M.A. (C.R.C.S., 1975).

The Principles and Practice of Astrology Noel Tyl.

Heaven Knows What Grant Lewi.

Astrology, A Cosmic Science Isabel Hickey.
Saturn: A New Look at an Old Devil Dr Liz Greene (Aquarian Press, 1977).

As you'll observe when browsing through bookshops, there are literally hundreds of books, old and new, on the subject of astrology. Avoid the 'pop' type which are usually written by authors without genuine qualifications. Always look at the book jacket and cover information which should state the author's background and experience.

Personally, I most enjoy works by university-trained writers, such as Tyl and Arroyo, both psychologists with excellent qualifications from American universities. Liz Greene holds a doctorate as well. None of these are 'heavy' writers so their books are interesting and easy to understand, once you've thoroughly absorbed your basic training in astro-analysis as set out in these pages.

COMMUNICATING WITH CLIENTS

Even if you only plan to use your training to astro-analyse your family and friends, the moment you take another person's horoscope chart in your hands, you are cast in the role of professional counsellor and the other in the role of client. Remind yourself regularly of this but take care, too, it doesn't go to your head!

Every so often one hears shattering tales of astrologers dressing up (like mediaeval wizards) in star-strewn robes, gazing into crystal balls and decking the walls of their consulting rooms with weird pictures or magical symbols. This off-beat behaviour is very off-putting to clients, many of whom (even if family or friends) are likely to be nervous anyway.

To illustrate: I once had a small tea urn in my city consulting rooms which, when heating, gave out a somewhat unnerving wailing sort of noise. One morning, a client arrived early. As I ushered him into my office, I apologized for the strange sounds. 'Oh,' he said, looking both troubled and rather sheepish, 'I thought it was . . . well, kind of background music!'

This little anecdote acts as a reminder of the fact that many laymen, despite mountains of evidence to the contrary, still secretly believe astro-analysis is linked with spiritualism, incantations and other occult practices.

So take care you do nothing to foster this totally false belief, even if you only have a corner of the house to work and discuss charts in, strive to keep the atmosphere professional, pleasant and reassuring.

The mention of family made in the first paragraph of this section is worth stressing. You can gain penetrating insight into the motivations of your partner and family members by means of the astro-analytical techniques you have learnt in this course. Many a tottering relationship has been rescued by each party's deepened understanding of the needs of each other. Faults are more easily tolerated, clashes more quickly overcome if you both know why they exist.

The same goes for your children. In some stages of my own life—and despite my prior training as a psychologist—I know there would have been more fur flying in more directions in battles of wills between my three daughters and myself (especially in their teenage years) without the help of astrology. But because I had their charts in hand, I was able to see them as people and thus avoid the hand-wringing uncertainties of childhood, and the blood-and-thunder clashes of adolescence.

Coping with sceptics, scoffers and Doubting Thomases

From the moment you become seriously involved on astro-analysis, you'll run across strays from all the above-mentioned categories. Don't be disheartened or hurt when such types set out to rubbish your science and you. If questioned, you'll find not one of them has ever opened a serious astrology text. And secondly, you'll observe, beneath the verbal outburst, an element of fear. These people don't want to know about themselves, don't want to hear the home truths of astro-analysis because they might have to do something about themselves.

The horoscope chart will not permit anyone to cherish false illusions! Personally, I never try to convert those who block their ears. Everyone comes to astrology *when* they are ready for what it can teach them.

But if you're interested in further reading on why the science works and the scientific evidence on which its doctrines are based, read *The Case for Astrology,* by John West and Jan Toonder.

At the other end of the scale, once you become proficient in astro-analysis, you'll also need to protect yourself against an invading army of friends and acquaintances who *do* want to pour out their troubles to you but *don't* want to take your advice or anyone else's. This is a palpable waste of your time and theirs. (Remember what Hippocrates said!) And before long, you'll feel astrology has become, in the words of a long-time practitioner colleague of mine, 'an albatross around your neck'.

In the Doubting Thomas category, you'll meet those who protest that they are not quite as you have analysed them. Never thrust your conclusions down anyone's throat—merely ask them to reflect more deeply on specific points—because we all tend to repress experiences or needs which don't match up to our self-image.

I well recall one female client, with many planets in Leo and a tough fourth house, insisting she had had a very happy childhood. Later in the discussion, she admitted her mother had been a hopeless alcoholic who nearly every day would leave her little girl in the street outside hotels until the police arrived to take the tearful and desperate child home to her father. This was, of course, a frightening experience for the proud, love-seeking Lion personality, so she had painfully built up a protective fantasy about her early years. Yet the deep hurt was still festering in the psyche, damaging her adult relationships, and it would continue to do so until she dragged it out from the depths, confronted it and thus destroyed its power.

Remember this sad little story when you face someone who says to you. 'Oh, no! That's not really me!' If you have got your analysis right, your comment won't be wrong. Probe gently and more deeply and the answer will be there.

On the other side of the coin, you'll sometimes meet a couple who want you to analyse their personalities one after the other. It's often amusing to hear, a wife interrupt with. 'John's not like that!' Whereupon John says 'Oh, yes, I am!' This an example of failure by one party to move past the projected personality or mask of the other.

Hail and farewell

In these concluding paragraphs, I'd like to use that Ancient Roman accolade, which, if I remember my Latin correctly, reads: *Ave Atque Vale*.

'Hail!' to you, as a fellow-traveller along the road that leads to greater self-awareness and personal fulfilment—through studying the techniques of astro-analysis. 'And Farewell!'

In this book, I have sought to concentrate all the knowledge and experience I have gained since I first qualified as a psychologist at the age of twenty-one and as an astrologer many years later. I have done everything I can to make it easy, cutting out the non-essentials and teaching you how to use astrology as all psychologist-astrologers do: without vagueness, negativity or unscientific methods in chart assessment and counselling others.

In adding test exercises and model answers to important chapters of the course, you have the chance to check your progress and winkle out mistakes before they become habits.

So now, it's over to you! Good luck and good charting!

INDEX

Other recommended reading . . .

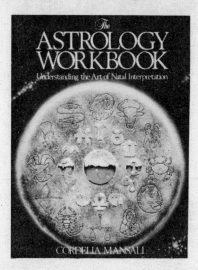

THE ASTROLOGY WORKBOOK

Cordelia Mansall

For anyone who wishes to learn the ground rules of modern astrology, this book provides the ideal starting point. A tutor with the Faculty of Astrological Studies since 1977, Cordelia Mansall has used her experience of teaching astrology to beginners to produce a manual that takes a fresh and original approach to the problem of understanding astrological concepts and techniques. In a clear and accessible style, THE ASTROLOGY WORKBOOK explains the first principles of astrology and gives full instructions on how to construct, analyze and interpret a birth chart. It also considers:
★ the growth and development of astrology
★ the symbolism of the zodiac
★ the houses and their meanings
★ the significance of the planets
★ how to interpret aspects and harmonics

A Step-by-Step Guide
to Compatibility
in Relationships

M. E. Coleman BA, LL.B

A comprehensive, easy-to-
understand and informative blend
of psychology and astrology that
reveals what really makes — or
breaks — sexual relationships

ASTRO-PICK YOUR PERFECT PARTNER

M. E. Coleman

What makes you fall in love and out of it? How can you tell the difference between sexual attractions and long-term caring? Does loving someone mean you can overcome incompatibility of life styles and upbringing? Can you handle lifetime commitment or can't you? Today, these are the questions that everyone worries and wonders about as drastic social changes alter the meaning of marriage, morals, and even the definition of love itself. This book can help you find the answers to all your relationship problems. Written by a university-qualified psychologist, it shows you how to assess accurately and quickly your own special needs in love and sex, then how to rate their compatibility with those of your existing or intended partner. The technique is called astro-analysis because it merges the interpretation of personality traits shown in the horoscope chart with modern methods of psychological analysis. As you work with it, you'll discover facets and drives in your own nature you didn't know existed. You'll see those you care most about in a new and revealing light. Easy-to-use Compatibility Rating Tables ensure you make no mistakes and come up with right answers every time!